Hear the Word
Encountering its life

John White
John Balchin
Roy Clements
Jack Kuhatschek
Stephen D. Eyre

Foreword by
Ian Coffey

Inter-Varsity Press

INTER-VARSITY PRESS
38 De Montfort Street, Leicester LE1 7GP, England

The chapters in this book have appeared elsewhere. Chapter 1
was published as a UCCF Booklet under the same name
© 1985 by Inter-Varsity Christian Fellowship of the USA.
Chapters 2 and 4 are taken from *Let the Bible Speak*, by John
Balchin © John F. Balchin, 1981. Chapter 3 is taken from
The Fight, by John White © Inter-Varsity Christian
Fellowship of the USA. Chapters 5 and 6 are from the UCCF
Booklet, *Word and Spirit*, by Roy Clements © Roy Clements,
1986. Chapter 7 was published as a booklet, *Quiet Time
Dynamics*, by Stephen D. Eyre © 1989 by Stephen D. Eyre.
All are used by kind permission of the authors and publishers.

First published in this form 1990

British Library Cataloguing in Publication Data
Hear the Word.
    1. Bible Hermeneutics
    I. White, John *1924 Mar. 5* –
220.601

ISBN 0-85110-857-1

Typeset in Great Britain by Avocet Robinson, Buckingham

Printed in Great Britain by Cox & Wyman Ltd, Reading

*Inter-Varsity Press is the book-publishing division of the
Universities and Colleges Christian Fellowship (formerly the
Inter-Varsity Fellowship), a student movement linking
Christian unions in universities and colleges throughout the
United Kingdom and the Republic of Ireland, and a member
movement of the International Fellowship of Evangelical
Students. For information about local and national activities
write to UCCF, 38 De Montfort Street, Leicester LE1 7GP.*

Contents

Foreword

I can still recall singing, in far-off days in a Sunday School somewhere, a children's song which had the line, 'The best book to read is the Bible'. I have long since forgotten the rest of the song apart from that one line which remains firmly rooted in my memory. Much water has flowed under this particular bridge since then, but I have reached the conclusion that however trite and simplistic that little phrase may sound today, it is absolutely true.

Anyone wishing to live in God's world in God's way must soak themselves in God's Word. Joshua – chosen as successor to Moses – was given the unenviable task of leading the nation of Israel. The job called for extraordinary skills. He needed to be a political statesman, a military commander and a spiritual leader. When God called him to the task he gave him the secret of success: 'Do not let this Book of the Law depart from your mouth; meditate on it day and night, so that you may be careful to do everything written in it. Then you will be prosperous and successful' (Joshua 1:8).

We need that same commitment to imbibe Scripture if we are going to be effective as disciples of Christ in our generation. The content of our Bible has, of course, greatly expanded from the first five books of Moses (the Law) that Joshua was encouraged to diligently study. But the principle that lies behind this instruction holds true that 'man does not live on bread alone but on every word that comes from

5

the mouth of the Lord' (Deuteronomy 8:3). The Bible is inspired by God (literally, 'God-breathed', 2 Timothy 3:16) which places it as a book above all books in its power and influence.

It is my privilege to introduce *Hear the Word* to you. The book is made up of some collected writings of a group of Christian teachers who are united in the conviction that the Bible is the inspired Word of God and that its message must be correctly understood, taught and applied. Through these chapters, they tackle a number of difficult yet important questions:

- What does it mean to claim the Bible is 'inspired'?
- Is the Bible reliable — or does it contain errors?
- Haven't modern scientific discoveries disproved the Bible?
- How does God speak to people through Scripture?
- How do we interpret the Bible's message in today's world?
- What are the best methods of studying Scripture?
- What is the relationship between the Bible and the gift of prophecy today?
- How can I, as an individual, discover a deeper relationship with God through the pages of the Bible?

I have enjoyed reading what these gifted writers have to say in answer to these questions and I have been made aware once again of the sheer power of the Bible. Hardly surprising when we recall what Scripture says about itself — 'for the word of God is living and active' (Hebrews 4:12).

We are living in exciting and demanding days. At such a time as this the church of Jesus Christ needs to be known as 'the people of the Book', knowing how to read and interpret the signs of the times in the light of God's unchanging Word. History proves that the church is strong when our hold on Scripture is strong. In the words of St Augustine:

> The faith will totter if the authority of the Holy Scriptures loses its hold on men.
>
> We must surrender ourselves to the authority of Holy Scripture, for it can neither mislead nor be misled.

I am happy both to introduce and commend this book in the belief that, as we grasp hold of the message of the Bible and allow it to grasp hold of us, our lives – and ultimately our society – will be changed for the better.

Ian Coffey
Field Director
Evangelical Alliance of Great Britain

How to study the Bible

JACK KUHATSCHEK

SEVERAL years ago a well-known newspaper ran an advertisement of a new title, *How to Read a Book*. Under the picture of a puzzled adolescent reading a letter were these words:

How to read a love letter

This young man has just received his first love letter. He may have read it three or four times, but he is just beginning. To read it as accurately as he would like, would require several dictionaries and a good deal of close work with a few experts of etymology and philology. However, he will do all right without them.

He will ponder over the exact shade of meaning of every word, every comma. She has headed the letter, 'Dear John.' What, he asks himself, is the exact significance of those words? Did she refrain from saying 'Dearest' because she was bashful? Would 'My Dear' have sounded too formal?

Maybe she would have said 'Dear So-and-So' to

anybody! A worried frown will now appear on his face. But it disappears as soon as he really gets to thinking about the first sentence. She certainly wouldn't have written *that* to anybody!

And so he works his way through the letter, one moment perched blissfully on a cloud, the next moment huddled miserably on a downer. It has started a hundred questions in his mind. He could quote it by heart. In fact, he will − to himself − for weeks to come.

The advertisement concludes: 'If people read books with anything like the same concentration, we'd be a race of mental giants.'[1]

The Bible is God's love letter to us. But if we want to experience the eagerness and intensity of the young man in the advertisement, we must learn how to study it on our own. This chapter presents the basic skills needed for studying the Bible. These skills are vitally important for both new Christians and those who have known Christ for many years.

The nature of Scripture

The Bible is unique. It is unlike any other book because God himself is the Author. Because the Bible is God's book, it is trustworthy − he makes no mistakes. It is authoritative − he has the right to rule over every part of our lives. And it is *eternal* − it speaks to people in every time, place, language and culture. It never loses its relevance; it is never out of date.

In another sense the Bible is not unique. Because it was also written by human authors, the Bible shares many similarities with other books. Like other non-fiction books the Bible is *historical* — it was first written to people in a particular time, place, language and culture. And like other books the Bible is *literature* — the authors communicated through stories, poems, letters and parables.

The historical, literary and eternal qualities of Scripture require us to follow three steps in studying and applying the Bible:

First, if we take the historical nature of Scripture seriously, we must learn something about the time, language, culture and geography of the biblical world. This will help us understand how God's Word spoke to those who first heard it.

Second, if we take the literary nature of Scripture seriously, we must acquire reading skills — the kind of skills required to understand any book. This will help us to understand what the author is saying.

Third, if we take the eternal nature of Scripture seriously, we will study the Bible carefully and prayerfully. This will help us to understand how God's Word speaks to us today.

Step one: Journeying into the past

In 1895 H. G. Wells wrote a book called *The Time Machine*. In it he describes a machine that could transport a person into the past or future:

> 'Now I want you clearly to understand that this lever, being pressed over, sends the machine gliding into the future, and this other one reverses the motion. This saddle is the seat of the time traveller. Presently I am going to press the lever, and off the machine will go. It will vanish . . .' We all saw the lever turn. I am absolutely certain there was no

trickery. There was a breath of wind, and the lamp flame jumped. One of the candles on the mantel was blown out, and the machine suddenly swung round, became indistinct, was seen as a ghost for a second perhaps, as an eddy of faintly glittering brass and ivory; and it was gone − vanished![2]

In a sense, studying the Bible is like entering a time machine. We must cross the barriers of time, language, culture and geography in order to understand the people of the Bible and the problems they were facing. This helps us grasp how God's Word applied to *their* situation.

Then, when we have understood how God's Word applied to the people of that century, we re-enter the time machine and return to the twentieth century. Now we are able to reflect on what we have learned and how it applies to our time and culture and the problems *we* face.

Our time machine is constructed from the various tools available to the modern student of the Bible. With these tools we can cross the barriers which separate us from the biblical world.

1. Crossing the time barrier

The events described in the Bible took place thousands of years ago. This creates one obvious problem for understanding these events − *we weren't there!* Therefore, we often lack important information regarding the historical context in which these events took place.

For example, almost every New Testament letter was written to address a particular problem or set of problems: the Galatians were seeking to be justified by law; the Corinthians wanted answers to questions about marriage, spiritual gifts, meat offered to idols and so on; Timothy needed to know how to restore order to a church.

12

Unless we understand these problems or questions, the letters are like listening to one end of a telephone conversation. We hear what the author is saying, but we don't know *why* he is saying it. The same is true when we read the Psalms and Prophets. We know only half of the story!

One way to learn about the historical context is to look for clues within the book or passage itself. For example, in 1 John we read, 'I am writing these things to you about those who are trying to lead you astray' (2:26). As we look elsewhere in the letter we discover that these false teachers had originally been part of the church: 'They went out from us, but they did not really belong to us' (2:19). John calls them 'antichrists' (2:18). There are many other statements, some explicit and some implicit, which give us additional details about the situation that John's readers faced and why he wrote to them.

Once you have looked within the book or passage itself, it is helpful to consult a Bible dictionary or handbook. For example, under the listing 'John, letters of' we can find further information about the historical context and purpose of 1 John.

It is also a good idea to read related passages in the Bible. For example, Psalm 51 was written by David after his adultery with Bathsheba. We can read about David and Bathsheba in 2 Samuel 11 – 12. (In Psalm 51 the heading over the psalm tells us why it was written. When such information isn't given, a Bible dictionary or commentary will often mention related passages.) Similarly, if we study the book of Philippians, we will want to consult the book of Acts, which provides information about the founding of the church at Philippi (Acts 16).

The more we know about the historical context of a biblical passage, the better equipped we will be to understand the message of the author. Such information can be like finding missing pieces of a puzzle. As they are put into place, the whole picture becomes much clearer.

2. Crossing the language barrier

The fact that the Bible was written in Hebrew, Aramaic and Greek instead of English creates a significant barrier to understanding its message. Anyone who tries to learn these languages quickly realizes how difficult they are to master. Fortunately, those who are experts in biblical languages have crossed this barrier for us (for the most part) by translating the biblical languages into modern English. In fact, there are numerous Bible translations to choose from.

There are literal translations such as the New American Standard Bible and the Revised Standard Version. There are dynamic-equivalent translations such as the New International Version, the Revised English Bible and the Good News Bible. And there are free translations such as the Living Bible and the New Testament in Modern English (J. B. Phillips).

Each type of translation has strengths and weaknesses. A literal translation follows the wording of the Hebrew or Greek as closely as possible, but such wording often sounds awkward in English.

A free translation is more concerned with clarity than exact wording. Such translations are easy to read but give the impression that the Bible was written in the twentieth century. For example, the word *lamp* might be translated as 'flashlight'!

Dynamic-equivalent translations are probably the best choice. They don't try to update matters of history or culture (a lamp is a lamp, not a flashlight). But they translate the biblical words and phrases into precise equivalents in English. As a result they are accurate and easy to read.

The smart Bible student will take advantage of all three types of translations. Each one provides unique insights into what the author originally said in his own language.

It is best, however, to use either literal or dynamic-equivalent translations such as the NIV, RSV and NASB as the basis of our study. These translations allow us to interpret the passage on our own rather than doing much of the work for us. Then, after we have grasped the basic meaning of the passage, a free translation can help to clarify further what the author is saying.[3]

3. Crossing the culture barrier

Even with a good translation there will be times when we will not understand the meaning of a word. For example, the words *justification, propitiation, reconciliation* and *redemption* are extremely important theologically but are unfamiliar to many Bible students. They are unfamiliar to us because they come from the language and culture of the biblical authors rather than from the language and culture of the twentieth century.

For example, why did Rachel steal her father's household gods (Gn. 31:19)? Why was Jonah so fearful of the Ninevites? Who were the Samaritans, and why was there such hatred between them and the Jews (Jn. 4:9)? What was the city of Corinth like, and what special temptations did the Corinthians face because they lived there? As we come to understand the answers to such questions, we receive new insight into the passage or book we are studying.

Imagine you are studying Amos and you come across the following verse. 'On the day I punish Israel for her sins . . . the horns of the altar will be cut off and fall to the ground' (Am. 3:14). This verse is meaningless to us in the twentieth century, but a Bible dictionary or encyclopaedia will help us understand what Amos meant. If we look up the word *altar* or *horn*, we discover that in Old Testament times many Jews believed the altar was a place of refuge. Both Adonijah and Joab took hold of the horns of the altar for protection (1 Kings 1:50; 2:28). Amos is warning that the Israelites will flee to the altar and find its horns (that is, their protection) are gone!

We can also discover a great deal about the culture simply from the book or passage being studied. For example, the Gospels are full of references to life in first-century Palestine. We know that the Jews were under Roman rule (Lk. 3:1) and expected the Messiah to come and free them from their enemies (Lk. 1:71). We read about the legalism and externalism of the religious authorities and how they hindered a true knowledge of God (Mt. 23). We also gain an understanding of everyday life in Bible times: business practices (Lk. 16:1–8), weddings (Jn. 2), funerals (Jn. 11), wages (Mt. 20:1–16), taxes (Mt. 22:15–22) and so on. It is impossible to study the Bible without becoming immersed in ancient Middle Eastern culture. As we become more familiar with this culture, we are better able to cross this barrier between our world and theirs.

4. Crossing the geographical barrier

Some people are fortunate enough to visit the Holy Land. When they return, they report that the Bible comes to life in ways they have never experienced. Those of us who have not visited the Holy Land can also have this experience in a more limited way. As we learn about biblical geography, many Bible passages take on new meaning.

For example, in Amos 1:3–2:16 the prophet condemns Damascus, Gaza, Tyre, Edom, Ammon, Moab, Judah and Israel. At first it may seem that Amos mentions these cities and nations at random, but a closer examination reveals otherwise. The first three are the capitals of heathen nations unrelated to Israel. The next three are blood relatives of Israel. Judah, the seventh, is Israel's brother nation of the south. Finally, Israel itself is named.

The effect on Amos's audience would have been staggering. The Israelites would have cheered at his judgments against the heathen nations. But as his words came closer and closer to home – Ammon, Moab, Judah – they would have begun to sweat. With the words. 'For three sins of Israel, even for four, I will not turn back my wrath.' They were caught in Amos's 'coil of condemnation'.

There are several ways to become familiar with biblical geography. Many Bibles include maps for the reader to consult. A good Bible atlas or Bible dictionary can also supply valuable information about unfamiliar places. These sources can help us trace the route of the Exodus, show us the cities conquered by Joshua and identify Israel's neighbouring enemies. They can allow us to follow the ministry of Jesus and the missionary journeys of Paul. We can learn the location of the New Testament churches and how their location may have influenced their life and culture. If we consult these sources whenever we come across an unfamiliar location in the Bible, they can help us cross the geographical barrier.

Step two: Learning to read

Imagine that you have entered the time machine and have completely crossed the barriers of time, language, culture and geography. You are in Corinth in the first century. You are dressed in Greek clothes. You speak Greek fluently and know the surrounding culture and geography. You are even a member of the church at Corinth and are intimately acquainted with the people and problems in the church.

As you are gathering for worship in a nearby home, a messenger comes to the door with a letter from Paul, the letter we now call 1 Corinthians. You unroll the scroll and begin reading the letter (in Greek, of course!). Does the fact that you have successfully crossed the barriers of time, language, culture and geography mean that you will automatically understand what Paul is saying? Not necessarily.

The apostle Peter was one of Paul's contemporaries and still found some things in his letters 'hard to understand' (2 Pet. 3:16). Of course Peter's difficulty may have been that *Paul* was unclear in places. But even when Paul writes clearly, our success in understanding him (or any other author) will depend on how skilful we are at reading. One aspect, therefore, of learning how to study the Bible focuses on acquiring reading skills — the kinds of skills that will help us whether we are reading the Bible, a novel, a magazine or a newspaper.

In order to read with understanding we need to concentrate on answering one primary question: What did the author mean to convey to his original readers? (The question of what the passage means to us today will be covered in the section on returning to the present.) You can discover the meaning of the author by following five guidelines:

- Identify the type of literature you are studying.
- Get an overview of the book.
- Study the book passage by passage.
- Be sensitive to the mood of the book or passage.
- Compare your interpretation with one or two good commentaries.

1. Identify the type of literature you are studying [4]

A cult expert was giving a lecture one evening on Mormonism. A few Mormons heard about the lecture and decided to attend. About half way through the meeting, one of them stood up and began arguing that God the Father has a physical body like ours. He 'proved' his point by referring to passages which refer to God's 'right arm', 'hand', 'eyes' and so on. The cult expert asked him to read aloud Psalm 17:8. 'Hide me in the shadow of your wings.'

'But that is simply a figure of speech,' protested the Mormon.

'Exactly,' replied the speaker.

The biblical authors communicated in a variety of ways – through stories, letters, poems, proverbs, parables, metaphors and symbols. Each type of literature has its own unique features. We must identify the type of literature and language an author is using in order to interpret his meaning correctly. If we assume he is speaking literally when he is speaking metaphorically (the mistake made by the Mormon), we end up with nonsense.

The literature of the Bible has been classified into various types. They include:

Discourse. Discourse is a logical and extended discussion of a subject. The New Testament letters are the clearest examples of discourse. Some of the prophetic sermons and the longer sermons of Jesus also fall into this category.

Prose narrative. This is the style used in books such as Genesis, Joshua and the Gospels. The author describes and re-creates scenes and events from biblical history that are theologically significant.

Poetry. The Psalms, of course, fit into this category. Biblical poetry uses figurative language, different types of parallelism and is emotional in nature.

Proverbs. Proverbs, such as those in the book of Proverbs, are wise sayings. They are practical *principles* for living. They should not be confused with commands or promises.

Parables. Jesus used parables more than anyone else in Scripture. A parable explains a spiritual truth by means of a story or analogy. It is an extended simile or metaphor.

Prophetic literature. The prophetic books include the four major prophets (Isaiah, Jeremiah, Ezekiel and Daniel) and the twelve minor prophets (Hosea, Joel and Amos to Malachi). The prophets were spokesmen for God who announced the curses and blessings associated with God's covenant with Israel.

Apocalyptic literature. The books of Daniel and Revelation are a special type of prophecy known as apocalyptic literature. The word *apocalypse* means to 'uncover' or 'reveal' something which is hidden. One distinct feature of these books is their heavy use of symbols.

Once you have identified the type of literature you are studying, consult a Bible dictionary. (If you haven't caught on by now, a Bible dictionary is a valuable tool to own.) For example, if you are studying the Psalms, it would be wise to read an article on Hebrew poetry in order to learn how it is put together. Likewise, if you are studying Revelation, read an article on apocalyptic literature. It will explain why this kind of literature seems so strange to us and will offer suggestions for interpreting it correctly.

2. Get an overview of the book

On a large windswept plain in Peru, archaeologists discovered a vast series of strange lines covering an area thirty-seven miles long. The archaeologists first thought these lines were ancient roads. Their true significance was not discovered until the men flew over the area in an aeroplane. The lines joined to form a design, an immense mural that could only be seen from high above.

In finding what the author meant to convey to his original readers, an overview helps us in two ways. First, it enables us to discover the main *theme* of the book as we observe repeated ideas. For example, the author of Hebrews emphasizes Christ's superiority. 'So he became as much superior to the angels as the name he has inherited is superior to theirs' (1:4). 'Jesus has been found worthy of greater honour than Moses' (3.3). 'We have a great high priest' (4:14).

Second, an overview helps us discover the *structure* of the book — how the parts of the book contribute to the overall theme. The structure of Hebrews clearly demonstrates the superiority of Christ:

  a. Christ is superior to the prophets (1:1−3).
  b. Christ is superior to the angels (1:4−2:18).
  c. Christ is superior to Moses (3:1−4:13).
  d. Christ is superior to Aaron (4:14−10:18).
  e. Christ is superior as the new and living way to God (10:19−12:29).

The structure of a book will be closely related to its literary type. An epistle such as Hebrews is organized around ideas. Historical narratives can be structured in a variety of ways: Genesis (after chapter 11) is organized around people (Abraham, Isaac, Jacob and Joseph); Exodus is structured around geographical locations and events (in Egypt, *en route* to Sinai and at Sinai). The poetry of Psalm 119 is structured around the letters of the Hebrew alphabet!

The theme and structure of a book are the author's tools for accomplishing his *purpose* (see the section 'Crossing the time barrier'). For example, because the 'Hebrews' were being persecuted for their faith in Christ, they were tempted to forsake Christianity and return to Judaism. The author emphasizes how foolish and serious this would be since Christ is far superior to anyone or anything Judaism offered.

An overview is like looking through a zoom lens. Begin with a panoramic view through the lens by reading quickly through the book, trying to discover repeated ideas or words that tie the book together. When it isn't possible to read the entire book, skim through its contents, paying particular attention to chapter or paragraph headings in your Bible.

Now zoom in closer by looking for major sections or divisions within the book. Each section will focus primarily on one subject. Once you have discovered that subject, try to summarize it by giving a brief title to the section. Now you are ready to focus on the details of the landscape — the paragraphs, sentences and words.

At each step of the way look for connections or relationships between the sections and paragraphs. For instance, if we were studying Romans, we would find that 1:18 – 3:20 describes the *need* of humanity; then 3:21 – 5:21 shows God's *solution* to that need. Romans 7:7 – 8:39 contrasts the death that comes through sin (7:7–25) with the life that comes through Christ and his Spirit (8:1–39). As an author progresses from one paragraph or section to another, he might move from problem to solution, cause to effect, general to specific, as well as using comparison, contrast, repetition and so on. We can become alert to these links in his chain of reasoning by asking ourselves how each section relates to the next and how it contributes to the overall argument of the author.

The more times we read a book, the more familiar we will become with its theme and structure. Our original overview will help us to understand the whole of the book. This understanding will tend to affect the way we interpret its parts. But as we gain familiarity with the *parts*, our understanding of the whole may need to be modified, and so on. Each time we go through this cycle, we will come closer and closer to grasping the meaning of the author.

3. Study the book passage by passage

Once you have an overview of the theme and structure of a book, begin studying it passage by passage. In our modern Bibles a passage can be a paragraph, a group of paragraphs or a chapter. Realize, however, that the Bible did not originally contain chapters, paragraphs or verses (or even punctuation!). These are helpful additions to our Bibles, but we need not be bound by them.

As we study a passage, we should seek to understand its content and its context.

We discover the *content* of a passage by reading and rereading it. As we read we must first ask ourselves, 'What is the main subject of the passage?'

For example, love is obviously the subject of 1 Corinthians 13 since the word (or pronouns referring to it) occurs seventeen times in only thirteen verses. But love is a broad subject, one which Paul might have looked at from a hundred different perspectives.

Therefore, the second thing we must ask is, 'What did Paul say about love?' A closer look at the chapter reveals the following:

a. Love is superior to spiritual gifts because without love all gifts are meaningless (13:1–3).
b. Love is superior to spiritual gifts because of its selfless qualities (vv.4–7).
c. Love is superior to spiritual gifts because it endures for ever (vv.8–13).

We should also pay attention to the *context* of the passage by reading the verses or paragraphs immediately before and after it. Ask, 'Why is this passage here? How does the author use it to make his point clearer?'

Many people, for example, read 1 Corinthians 13 without considering how it fits into Paul's overall argument. We find it is sandwiched between two chapters which talk about spiritual gifts. Therefore, Paul's discussion of love *in this context* must have something to do with the broader subject of gifts, as the outline above clearly indicates.

4. Be sensitive to the mood of the book or passage

The Bible is more than a collection of ideas. The biblical authors and characters were people like us with passions and feelings. Sorrow and agony permeate Jesus' experience in Gethsemane. Galatians radiates the heat of Paul's anger toward the Judaizers and his perplexity over the Galatians. Psalm 148 is bursting with praise. While this is a more subjective aspect of Bible study, it can give us rich insights into the feelings and motivations of the biblical authors or characters. This in turn will add depth to our understanding of what they are saying.

5. Compare your interpretation with one or two commentaries

Once you feel you have understood the main subject of the passage and what the author is saying about it, compare your interpretation with that of one or two good *commentaries*. Commentaries can give you additional insights which you might have missed. They can also serve as a corrective if you have misunderstood something the author has said. But do your best to understand the passage on your own before consulting commentaries.

Step three: Returning to the present

Now we are ready to re-enter the time machine and return to the twentieth century. As we travel from the biblical world back to our own, we will seek to apply God's Word to our time and culture, using language that is meaningful to us today.

The eternal nature of Scripture should cause us to apply the Bible *carefully* and *prayerfully*.

In 2 Timothy 2:7 Paul writes to his young associate: 'Reflect on what I am saying, for the Lord will give you insight into all this.' Notice the two halves of this verse. First, Paul exhorts Timothy to *think* about what he has said. Studying and applying the Bible requires thought and reflection. We should handle the Scriptures carefully, using all of the tools and resources God has given us for understanding his Word. Only then can we be confident that we are applying the Scriptures in the way God intends. If we rush through our Bible study, we may end up hanging an applicational elephant from an interpretive thread.

Second, Paul tells Timothy it is God who grants understanding. Therefore, we must also handle the Bible prayerfully, asking the Author of Scripture to grant us understanding in everything. He must open our eyes to see clearly what he is saying. He must reveal those areas of our lives that need to be transformed by his Word and his Spirit. The psalmist writes, 'Open my eyes that I may see wonderful things in your law' (Ps. 119:18). The Lord is the revealer of Scripture.

To apply the Scriptures properly, we must remember what was said earlier about the nature of Scripture. Almost every book of the Bible was written to address specific problems, needs and questions of the people living *at the time*. For example, the Corinthians had problems of division, immorality and lawsuits among believers. They also had questions about marriage, food sacrificed to idols and spiritual gifts. Paul wrote 1 Corinthians to address their specific problems and to answer their specific questions.

We face many of these same problems and questions

today. It is still possible to take a fellow believer to court, and we still have questions about marriage. In fact, there are hundreds of ways in which our problems and needs correspond to those faced by the people in the Bible. This is natural since we share a common humanity.

This leads us to the first principle of application: *Whenever our situation corresponds to that faced by the original readers, God's Word to us is the same as it was to them.*

But there are also situations from ancient times that do not have an exact counterpart today. This, too, is to be expected because of the differences between modern and biblical cultures. For example, no-one in our society sacrifices food to idols.

In such cases we should follow the second principle of application: *Whenever our situation does not correspond to that faced by the original readers, we should look for the principle underlying God's Word to them. We can then apply that principle to comparable situations today.* [5]

What was the principle underlying Paul's words about food sacrificed to idols? He was concerned that the Corinthians should not do anything that would lead someone with a weak conscience to sin: 'Therefore, if what I eat causes my brother to fall into sin, I will never eat meat again, so that I will not cause him to fall' (1 Cor. 8:13). This principle might be applicable to many situations today, such as whether a Christian should drink alcoholic beverages around someone who is a former alcoholic − or whether to drink at all.

Once we understand these principles of application, we will find unlimited ways in which God's Word applies today. We can ask such question as:

- Is there a command for me to obey?
- Is there a promise to claim?

- Is there an example to follow?
- Is there a sin to avoid or confess?
- Is there a reason for thanksgiving or praise?
- What does this passage teach me about God, Jesus Christ, myself, others?

Practice makes perfect (well, almost)

Learning to study the Bible is like learning any other skill – the more we do it, the easier it becomes. At first, following the steps outlined in this chapter may seem mechanical, like learning how to type. But after a while, many of these steps will seem much more natural, almost automatic. And remember, we are not alone in Bible study. The Holy Spirit did not write Scripture in order to confuse us. He will help us understand and apply the Bible as we pray, study diligently and make use of many of the study aids available today. *Bon appetit!*

Notes

1. As quoted by Robert A. Traina, *Methodical Bible Study* (Wilmore, Ken.: Asbury Theological Seminary, 1952), pp. 97–98.

2. H. G. Wells, *The Time Machine* (New York: Bantam Books, 1982), pp. 9–10.

3. What about the King James Version? It is beautifully written, but I would not recommend it for Bible study. A good translation should cross the language barrier between the biblical world and our own. The KJV did that for those living in the seventeenth century, but for those of us today, methinks a four-hundred-year gap doth create unnecessary confusion!

4. This point is expanded in chapter 4.

5. For a fuller discussion of the principles of application see

Gordon D. Fee and Douglas Stuart, *How to Read the Bible for All Its Worth* (London: Scripture Union, 1983), pp. 57–71.

The book that is different

J O H N   B A L C H I N

THAT pioneer translator of the New Testament into modern English, J. B. Phillips, tell us that although he tried to remain emotionally detached from his work, 'I found again and again that the material under my hands was strangely alive'.[1] It was rather like rewiring an old house where the electricity had not been turned off! There was something 'uncanny' about the Bible books.

What is it about the Bible which makes it different from the other great works of literature? As we have seen, it *is* literature, but is it more than just a human creation? What was it that drew this collection of assorted manuscripts together in the first place, so that Jews and then Christians claimed that it was one book and not many? After all, that is what they were assuming when they compared harder passages with easier ones when trying to understand them; that it was not just some books but *a* book, and then not just *a* book but *the* Book, God's book in fact.

There have been some who have claimed that it is unfair to come to the Bible like this. We ought to come, they say, 'with an open mind', confining ourselves to the objective study of a piece of literature. This sounds fine, but an 'open mind' is, in fact, a myth! When we start assessing Scripture, or anything else come to that, we all have certain ideas already in our minds, what we call a 'pre-understanding', which colours all our conclusions.

For example, if we do not believe in the supernatural, we shall set about explaining away anything which claims to be supernatural in natural terms. If we do not believe that God was behind the writing of the Bible, we shall look at it as a random collection of human literature.

What is 'inspired'?

Now it is reasonably obvious that what we call the Bible was originally a collection of books written by different people at different times. The result ought to have been diverse in the extreme, but both Jews and Christians recognized that they all had something in common. They believed that the Bible was 'inspired', that it was, in the final analysis, the product of the mind of God himself.[2]

When we speak about the 'inspiration' of Scripture in this way, we are using the word in a particular sense. We are speaking about that miracle whereby God took up the authors in the totality of their personalities, and caused them to write as they did. This is far more than inspiration in the usual literary sense of the word. When we say, 'The Bible is inspired,' we mean something rather different than when we say, 'Shakespeare was inspired,' or 'Tolstoy was an inspired author'. In their cases we are speaking about their literary genius which enabled them to write as they did. In the case of the Bible authors, we are claiming that God decided to commit truth about himself and his ways to objective written form, and that he used them to this end.

'Thus says the Lord'

This is certainly what they themselves claimed with almost monotonous regularity. 'Thus says the Lord' or 'the Word of the Lord' are phrases that occur again and again in the Old Testament, and the New Testament writers assumed an authority which was no less. We may, of course, argue that a claim to inspiration in this sense does not necessarily constitute the genuine article. Many in the past, as well as today, have claimed that they were God's spokesmen, but their contradictory voices and lives have told otherwise. I know a fellow who claims to be a prophet in his own group. He *claims* to have a particular insight into God's will for the others, and because they accept his claims, his word has become law. But somehow what he says and how he lives do not add up. I am not prejudging the issue of prophecy today; all I know is that the way in which this man behaves at times is considerably different from what I read about Christian leadership in the New Testament.

Christ as the key

The key to our understanding of biblical inspiration, the linchpin on which it all hangs, is a rather different person, Christ himself.

There can be no argument that Jesus assumed and built upon the idea that the Bible was inspired. In this respect he was one with the Jews of his own time. For him, the Old Testament recorded what God had revealed of himself to man, not simply in general terms, but in specific details. He could appeal to the very words of the Old Testament writers as having God's authority, and therefore as being above contradiction.[3] So, inspiration and Jesus Christ's personal authority go together. You cannot have the one without the

31

other. When we say that Scripture is inspired, we are really only taking the claims of Christ seriously.[4]

Apostolic authority

One might say a similar thing about the New Testament writings. As with the Old Testament, the writers simply assume that what they have to say is God's Word with God's authority.[5] It seems that even in New Testament times some of their writings were given a status alongside the Old Testament,[6] and the very collection of them tells us that Christians rapidly became 'a people of the Book' like the Jews before them. For the early believers these books and letters spoke with the delegated authority of Christ as did no others — and there were others to choose from, some bearing the names of apostles who were supposed to have written them. There was a vibrance and a vitality about the twenty-seven which we have today which attracted support from Christians everywhere. These were the books which spoke to them in the same accents of Christ himself.

Was Jesus wrong?

Some have argued that the whole idea of Scripture is unnecessary for the Christian faith.[7] Others have tried to maintain that Christ's attitude to Scripture was simply part of his self-limitation; that in becoming man, the Son of God became human to the point of being a child of his own time, limited in outlook so that he accepted what to us are unacceptable and dispensable ideas. But this is to question the very basis on which the Christian faith is built. If Christ was wrong on this point — and he seems to give considerable weight to it — how can we be sure that he was right on any point?

We are left to our own subjective devices, selecting what appeals to us from Christ's teaching and the Bible generally.

In a word, we construct our own religion and way of life, but it cannot be said that we have taken Christ and his authority seriously.

Modern views

The bane of modern theology which has largely dispensed with the idea of inspiration is its sheer subjectivity. Read half a dozen different theology books and you end up with half a dozen different gospels or even half a dozen different Christs. Some aspect of the New Testament message which may appeal to one person as important carries no weight at all with the next. This then filters down through our colleges to our church pulpits and RE lessons where preachers and teachers tell us that 'it may be this or it may be that. The scholars are not agreed'. As a result, the ordinary person does not know who or what to believe.

I am not unaware of the many problems involved in understanding the Bible, but, along with a good number of others, I prefer simply to start with Scripture and the idea of inspiration where Christ did.

Let us not be so naïve as to think that we are the first generation which has seen difficulties in approaching the Bible in this way. The Jews themselves were also quite aware of a good number of the Old Testament problems, and yet they tenaciously held on to the divine over-ruling and consequent authority of those writings.

God's Son

In Christ and his absolute claims to authority, we have an endorsement of their views which we can dispense with *only if we dispense with him*. In insisting on the inspiration of Scripture, conservative evangelicals are confessing that, difficulties and problems notwithstanding, they will follow Christ.

To argue the authority of the Bible from the Bible in this way has seemed to some to be a circular argument. 'Why do I accept the authority of the Bible? Because the Bible says it is authoritative!' But this is to misrepresent the situation. We need a higher authority to validate its claims. The ultimate authority, of course, is God, and if Christ is God's Son as he claimed to be, that authority comes down to us through him and his teaching.

How do we know that Jesus was (and is) the Son of God? Not just because he or his followers might have claimed that to be so, but because God raised him from the dead. Now if you read what the New Testament teaches about that, you will find that the writers are not simply making a bald claim, but rather that they invite us to consider the eyewitness evidence for ourselves. The resurrection can be investigated historically. The apostles did not believe and preach that Christ had risen merely because they had somehow got the idea into their heads. Something had happened to them. They had seen Christ alive after his death. When Jesus was executed, they were broken men. They had nothing more to live or hope for. When he rose from the dead it revolutionized their whole attitude to life as well as marking him out from the rest of mankind.[8] What is more, it validated all his claims, which in turn provide a point of reference for any other claim to authority, including that of Scripture.

Little by little

Another important presupposition lying behind this particular approach is the contention that the Bible has *one theme*. Despite its detail, it tells from start to finish of God's saving action in Christ. The Old Testament prepares for his coming; the New Testament expounds it. This is no new idea. Augustine back in the fourth century said as much, and he was only reiterating the claims of the New Testament writers themselves, that the Old was being fulfilled before their eyes. [9]

A growing light

This introduces us to something else that we must bear in mind when we interpret the Bible. God did not reveal himself and all his ways at one go. God's self-revelation to his people was like light dawning and growing fuller as the years went by. We call this 'progressive revelation', and it is something of a safeguard. Whereas we can compare scripture with scripture, it must be in the context of a God-directed development. This is why, for example, it would be totally wrong to expect Abraham or David to behave as Christians before their time. They lived long before the revelation was complete. What is remarkable is that they lived as well as they did with the little light that they had. At the same time, what God did in them and through them prepared the way for the fuller revelation which was to follow. Hence Abraham's faith and David's deep spiritual longings both find their fulfilment in the New Testament Christ.

This does not mean that we are excusing the inconsistent behaviour of such people as Abraham and David. The Bible characters are described for us 'warts and all' as the fallible human beings that they were, and I am sure that God intended it that way for our encouragement! When evaluating their stories, we have to distinguish between what is simply descriptive and what is actually prescriptive or commanded. Sometimes what they did is an example to us of 'how not to do it'. I am told to follow the example of Abraham's faith but not of his polygamy! The unhappy effects of the latter tell me that he was adrift at this point.

35

When talking about 'progressive revelation' we must also be careful not to confuse it with the popular view of religious development, that of man's 'long search' for God. This is the evolutionary view of religion, which makes out that man has been seeking after spiritual realities, in terms of crude and primitive ideas at first, but ultimately refining his views into higher beliefs.

I had an RE master at school who confidently told us that all religion had evolved from animism and spiritism, the worship of the spirits, to polytheism, the worship of many gods. From this it became henotheism, which has one high god plus several others, and eventually monotheism, the worship of one god, which is where we were at! His conclusion, of course, was that Jesus and the Christian faith were just the latest step on the evolutionary ladder, which did not please those of us in the Christian Union one bit. Later on I came to learn that this approach underlay a good deal of the liberal estimate of Jesus in the nineteenth century. For many, then, Jesus was just the greatest and best believer who ever lived, the man who found God, and so on.

God steps in

Not only does this theory about religion fall down through inconsistent evidence — some very primitive peoples hold relatively high views of spiritual things — it turns the idea of 'revelation' on its head. From a biblical point of view it is always God who takes the initiative, stepping into history, coming and revealing himself to man in his need. [10] Unaided, man may express his longings and fears and may reflect something of the fact that he was originally made in God's image, but he can never come to God through his own efforts. Progressive revelation is not the story of man's religious development, but the account of God's successive

36

dealings with man, leading him out of his blindness and into the true light.

Anyway, for the working evangelist or minister all this talk about men and women groping after God seems like a bitter joke. It may be true in some parts of the world, but in my experience the ordinary person in the factory or the office generally could not care less about God. If anything, when confronted with spiritual realities, they run away rather than clamour for the truth. That kind of reaction has more to do with the Bible view of revelation than with religious evolution.

One book or many?

This idea that there is one theme as far as the Bible is concerned is not accepted by many modern scholars. For example, one has maintained, 'The unity of the New Testament is a problem only because of the dogma of a holy book.'[11] Partly because of the stress on the human side of Scripture, the fashion has been to talk about biblical theolog*ies* rather than biblical theolog*y*.

This means that we cannot say 'what the Bible teaches' on a particular subject, but only how Paul or John or some other writer saw it. Because we have a collection of books from a number of minds, almost as diverse as the local lending library, it is argued that they must inevitably diverge and disagree. Hence John can be set against Paul, Peter against Luke and so on.

Parts of the same picture

Now there is no question about the plural authorship of the Bible, nor can we overlook the fact that different authors expressed themselves in different ways. That, however, does not necessarily mean that they have to disagree with one another. It is equally possible to argue that their individual teachings are complementary, that they round out one another.

Truth is many-sided, and different situations such as those confronting the authors and prompting their work demanded a stress on different aspects of the one truth. There were times when God's people needed comforting, as we discover in many of the psalms; equally there were times when they needed warning, which is what we find in Amos or Malachi. There were those who needed to be reminded that salvation was by faith, as did the Galatians; there were others who needed teaching that faith must express itself in works, as the readers of James's letter. We also need reminding sometimes that some of the books in the Bible were written in far from ideal conditions. One wonders if some of our modern scholars would be quite so comprehensive and consistent if they had to do their work in prison or on some hazardous journey.

Only one gospel

To set the Bible authors against one another is really to overlook their own sense of oneness in their fidelity to what God had revealed to them about himself. When it came to the gospel, Paul could claim, 'Whether then it was I or they, so *we* preach and so you believed.'[12] Equally he could castigate any who veered from what he knew to be God-given truth.[13] The New Testament authors were not writing tongue-in-cheek when they spoke of '*the faith*' (not '*the faiths*') which was once for all delivered to the saints. They meant it, and if we are going to take them seriously, we must accept that in good faith.

Their job was to make Christ known. So we find them, each in his own way, passing on the same message, not a different one.

38

What about the problems?

All this is not to say that there are no problem areas when it comes to interpreting the Bible. On the contrary, with the Bible being – in human terms – a collection of writings addressed on particular occasions to men and women far removed from our time and culture, it is to be expected that at times we shall have difficulties in grasping what the authors wanted to pass on. Of course we can be so preoccupied with the problems that we can forget that there is plenty in the Bible which hardly needs interpretation. The message is clear and relates to human needs just like our own. There are also areas, texts and passages, however, with which we must grapple if we are to understand them.

Start with the obvious

As we have seen, we might find help in some cases by studying clearer passages on the same subject. To ask, 'What is Jeremiah saying at this point?' may be answered by asking, 'What else has he said on the same topic elsewhere?' Knowing what he has plainly taught on another occasion will mean that there are certain things which he *cannot* be saying, while at the same time it might throw light on our difficult verse or passage. With the proviso we have mentioned about different authors sometimes using the same word in different ways, we may similarly move from book to book within the canon.

For example, a good number begin their study of the second coming of Christ with the highly symbolic book of Revelation. It would be much wiser to start with those clear and unambiguous statements about Christ's return which we find elsewhere in the New Testament, and then to try to understand Revelation in the light of them. If we fail to do this we might find ourselves constructing our doctrine from obscure and difficult texts. This is what the Mormons have done with their practice of baptizing on behalf of those who have died. The verse they use to support this teaching is obscure in the extreme. [14] Nobody can yet be completely sure of what it means. What they do, moreover, is inconsistent with the plain statement of the gospel both in Paul's writings and elsewhere in the New Testament. Whatever it means, it cannot mean what they have taken it to mean, that is, that you must be baptized if you are going to be saved, and that if you are not, then someone else must be baptized on your behalf.

Set the scene

As we have seen, sometimes the answer to a biblical riddle comes from outside Scripture as we learn from some extra-biblical source something of the background against which the Bible was written. The temptation in this approach is to assume that the biblical writers must have reacted in the same way as their Jewish or even pagan 'opposite numbers'.

For example, the problem of Paul's personal background has long divided New Testament scholars. Was he a Jew of the Dispersion, reared in Tarsus cheek by jowl with pagan influences to which he consciously or unconsciously moulded his gospel? Or was he true to his Jewish heritage so that we may understand him better against the background of the Old Testament and rabbinic thought? Although he himself clearly claims the latter position, a number of scholars have opted for the former, even maintaining that as a result the Christian faith was set on a course divergent from what Jesus originally intended. When we actually get down to studying Paul's writings, however, we find more than any Jewish or pagan background could provide. We find claims, sometimes quite explicit, that God had done and revealed a new thing; that the Christian gospel was neither brushed-up Judaism nor borrowed paganism. While grateful for the research which has provided us with a knowledge of the religious climate of Paul's day, we must not forget that God can do something original when he chooses to.

When in doubt . . .

It is also a great temptation, when faced with a textual difficulty, to fill out the gaps with conjecture, to opt for one of the possibilities and to disregard the rest. We have to remember that conjecture is only conjecture and not inspired personal revelation. When weighing up the possibilities involved in interpreting an obscure passage, we will naturally feel that one explanation is more probable than the rest. This is perfectly legitimate if we remember that we are dealing with probabilities and not certainties.

At times it takes more courage to be frankly and reverently agnostic, to say that we do not understand this or that issue *yet*. That 'yet' is important, because we know from the story of the last 100 years that countless points of debate have been cleared up, not to say many hypotheses debunked, as fresh evidence has come to light. A 'suspense account' is no bad thing and may be the wisest course in the long run.

Take for instance, the two accounts of Judas Iscariot's death.[15] You may, of course, conclude that either one or both are in error. Or you may bend over backwards to try and square the one with the other. But not only is it difficult to see how they harmonize, it is equally irresponsible to dismiss one or the other out of hand. The fact is that our data are incomplete, whereas those who wrote the accounts stood considerably nearer to the event than we do. We may conjecture, but when all is said and done, we have to admit that we do not know for certain how things worked out.

Evangelicals find it very hard to do this. They have been reared always to have an answer for any and every question which might come their way. It is hard for them to say, 'I just don't know.' We need the honesty and humility to acknowledge that there are many things we do not understand at present.

Is the Bible ever wrong?

The source

There is no doubt that, for Jesus and the apostles, Scripture was authoritative because in some undefined manner it was inspired in its very wording. The way in which they were prepared to pin their arguments on the words themselves, rather than merely on the general truths contained in the Bible, is evidence of that. For them it was wholly trustworthy down to the very words as a source of information about God and his ways with men. The Reformers adopted the same attitude. Scripture was 'infallible' in that it never misled or deceived the honest inquirer. The negative side of this essentially positive assurance is, of course, that there are no mistakes in the Bible: that it is inerrant.

The interpretation

There is a sense in which we must qualify the Reformers' position. After all, an infallible source does not necessarily guarantee an infallible interpretation. We have seen this sadly illustrated for us in the acrimonious debates of the Confessional era when, as heirs to the Reformers, all the combatants accepted an infallible Bible. It is a little naïve to think that if we all believe in an infallible Bible, we shall all, of necessity, come to the same theological viewpoint. Conservative evangelicals today are united in their confidence in Scripture, but divided over such issues as baptism or covenant theology or the second coming of

Christ. Our interpretation of even an infallible Bible will depend on our background, experience, prejudices and expectations.

Inerrancy

The whole subject has recently come to the foreground of theological debate among evangelicals. They have asked again in what sense they can use terms such as infallible and inerrant for Scripture today. In some circles infallibility has generally been taken to mean inerrancy. Some, however, would argue for an infallible Bible which was not inerrant, a position sometimes called 'limited inerrancy'. As far as the great truths which are central to salvation are concerned, the Bible, they say, is infallible. But because the Bible authors were conditioned by their own contemporary world views, they wrote things which we know now are not true.[16] The other wing have replied that the Bible is not only without error in what it teaches, but also in what it touches. Hence we must pay attention to its descriptions of mankind and the universe, even though modern science would explain them rather differently. If it is true at one level, it must be true at all levels.[17]

Is it possible to speak about an inerrant Bible? It largely depends in what area you are asking that question. For example, when it comes to textual studies, in places it is still impossible to reconstruct the original with total confidence, despite all the work that scholars have done. Again, when it comes to style, the authors' use of their language ranges from the very good to the far from perfect. We could not use the Bible as a textbook for perfectly regular Hebrew, Aramaic or Greek grammar and syntax. (Try reading the Greek of Revelation!)

43

Science and the Bible

It is, however, at the so-called 'scientific' level that the battle has raged. How can we, with our twentieth-century views of the universe, derived from observation and research, abandon these views in preference to those which appear primitive and mistaken? In some respects this is only an aspect of the 'science versus religion' debate which has raged ever since T. H. Huxley crusaded Darwin's views against the church. It has led to the popular belief that science has disproved the Bible, despite the fact that in practice a good number of scientists are also Bible-believing Christians.

What is sometimes forgotten is that scientific language is descriptive, and that it reflects the limited viewpoint of the observer. The man with the electron microscope is going to describe the universe in a rather different way from the man who sees it only with the naked eye. But this does not invalidate the latter's conclusions. How many of us living well into the post-Copernican era still speak about the sun *rising*? We ought to talk about the earth rotating! Yet we know perfectly well what we mean, and from the point of view of an ordinary observer, the sun *does* rise. In that sense it is a perfectly valid description.

Scripture, like any other ancient document, contains what we can call archaic scientific descriptions. They are not necessarily invalid or erroneous; they are limited by the point of view of the observer. What is more, they are generally secondary to the message of Scripture. The Bible was never intended to be a handbook on astronomy, medicine or Hebrew grammar.

There is no inherent contradiction between pure science and religion. The one describes the universe as it finds it; the other explains it. The problems sometimes arise when the scientist turns philsopher and begins to explain the universe in a materialistic or mechanistic manner.

Do the accounts conflict?

A similar thing might be said about another area in the debate, the alleged historical discrepancies in the Bible. Take the resurrection appearances of Jesus. As we have said, those who saw him shared their experiences, and it is these that we have recorded for us in the gospels, Acts and letters. That they did see him, eat with him and talk with him comes across quite clearly, but it is not quite so straightforward when we try to piece the story together, asking the question, 'Who saw him when?' Our difficulties are largely due to the fact that we lack the viewpoint of the original observers. Even eyewitness accounts will often vary in detail, not because the individuals concerned were necessarily mistaken or self-deluded, but because different aspects of the event either appealed to them or were hidden from them. It is just not adequate, when faced with seemingly contradictory reports in the historical sections of the Bible, to dismiss one or both as in error. From their respective viewpoints, they may both be right. Even a secular historian will look for ways of harmonizing apparent discrepancies, including the possibility that his own interpretation might be wrong, before judging the text as mistaken or deliberately misleading.

This is why evangelicals have traditionally attempted to reconcile, for example, the gospel records or the books of Kings and Chronicles where the data available appears to be divergent; the so-called concordist approach. Changes sometimes happen because of what the author is aiming at. So details are sometimes omitted because they are irrelevant. The order may be changed because the chronology of the event may not be the most important thing for us to know.

And, of course, we have to remember that history sometimes does nearly repeat itself. 'It is a poor historian . . . who immediately accuses his sources of error and distortion on the assumption that *similar* incidents do not happen, rather than weighing up what is the most realistic explanation of the accounts as they stand.'[18]

This approach is infinitely more reasonable than that of the scholar who seizes on any apparent contradiction in order to dispose of the trustworthiness of the documents, rather like a lawyer disposing of hostile witnesses. Unfortunately some appear to reverse the dictum of the law-courts: 'Innocent until proved guilty.' It is the responsibility of the Bible historian to question the text in order to find out, as far as he is able, what exactly happened. It is quite another thing to approach the text with a scepticism which disbelieves anything until it can be proved true. As Prof. Howard Marshall says, 'In the absence of contrary evidence belief is reasonable.'[19] We were not there, and they were, or at least they were much nearer those who were.

Asking the right questions

It could be argued that, even if there were no debate about the trustworthiness of Scripture, 'inerrancy' would be the wrong word to use when we come to literature. It may be perfectly justified when applied to a telephone directory, but literature seems to be in a different category from this.

Style

It is in the essence of literature that the author has licence to use a wide variety of literary devices — words, phrases, allusions, conceptions — in order to achieve his end, and which he might never have intended to be taken at their face value. Every culture has in its linguistic inheritance a vast number of forms derived either from its own history or borrowed from other cultures, which have lost their original literal meaning, but which readily convey ideas. Our own language is full of them. If we were to be as wooden and unimaginative in our interpretation of English literature as some require us to be when handling Scripture, the result would be laughable.

In this respect it is of immense value to study the literary types (or *genres*) of the Bible authors' contemporaries when they are available to us. For example, although the New Testament writers turn the style of their letters to their own end, they do follow the basic epistolary form of their own day. They begin with a greeting, a thanksgiving and a prayer just like other letters of that time.

Facts and figures

Part of our problem might be that we are coming to the Bible with the wrong set of questions, questions which it was never intended to answer. They arise out of our own particular cultural and philosophical background, and make us force ancient literature into a twentieth-century mould. Those who wrote the books of the Bible were not always as concerned about the details which we have come to look for. They were not always as preoccupied with trying to present facts objectively as we are; they were just as interested in what they meant spiritually. They came to their subject with a trust in God and a confidence in the gospel which dictated a positive approach. Their concern was for the great truths which the world needed to know in order to be saved, not the exact numbers of Israelites killed in a battle or even the exact order of events in Jesus' ministry. As we have already maintained, their whole philosophy of life (and that includes the way they handled history) was somewhat different from our own. It was not inferior because of that. They were children of their day, most certainly; but we are children of ours, heirs to a godless generation which has exalted mankind and human reason. In our conceit we assume that we are right and they were wrong, but this is not a foregone conclusion.

Overdoing it

It is not only Modernists, who do not necessarily believe that the Bible is inspired, who fall into this trap. Evangelicals are sometimes just as guilty of asking the wrong set of questions. While it is not unreasonable to believe that the Bible accounts do not contradict one another, efforts to reconcile the details sometimes become ludicrous. One recent author, worried about the apparently differing records of Jesus foretelling Peter's betrayal, ended up with the cock crowing on not one or two but four occasions! It was the only way in which he felt that all the evidence fitted in. It did not seem to occur to him that the writers were probably far more concerned about Peter's fickle allegiance to Jesus than they were about the habits of Palestinian poultry!

Under God's Word

The reason there was a Reformation was that individuals felt that in the Bible they had found God's revealed truth, and that they had to submit themselves to that truth. The Bible in turn became 'the touchstone of truth' as they called it. Everything had to be weighed and measured by the Word of God, even religious traditions of long standing. If other views differed from the Bible, it was God's Word which pronounced judgment and not *vice versa*. In terms of life and belief they put themselves *under* the Word of God. 'Let

God be true though every man be false' was, for Calvin, the fundamental basis of all Christian thinking.[20] So convinced were they of this principle that even their approach to Scripture was conditioned by Scripture. Their 'pre-understanding' of the Bible itself was biblical. What do I mean by this?

The Bible by the Bible

Dr Jim Packer has pictured this process of interpretation as a spiral.[21] First the interpreter must go to the text of Scripture to learn from it the doctrine of Scripture. He must ask, as we have done, how Christ approached Scripture. From this understanding of the Bible, he then works out his rules for interpreting it. He then returns to the text of Scripture, applying these principles in order to understand Scripture better. This in turn will tell him more about the sort of book the Bible is. In the light of this he then adjusts his approach and returns to the text and so on. The method can be seen as a one-way system: from the biblical texts to the doctrine; from the doctrine to the method of interpretation; from the method back to the texts again. So by successive approximations, which Dr Packer calls 'a basic method in every science', the interpreter moves progressively closer to the truth underlying the text.

Thinking biblically

Many of our problems in interpretation arise from the fact that, although we may be professing Christians, we do not think biblically. With the hindsight of history we can see that even the Reformers were not entirely consistent. They also were indebted to their own times and culture. But if they failed it was not their fault, for it was certainly their intention to rediscover and apply biblical principles to every department of life. On the positive side, they did produce a whole new world view, which has been only slowly eroded over the years and of which traces still remain in western culture.

The challenge to us is to do a similar thing in our own generation. Unfortunately we unconsciously accept the values, standards, outlooks and methods of Western atheistic materialism. Take, for instance, Christian parents' ambitions for their children. How many want their offspring to get a 'good' job (= well-paid), with 'decent prospects' (= promotion and more money)? How many have woken up to the fact that in biblical terms it does not matter what they do, where they go or whom they marry *as long as they are in God's will*? How many really believe that 'godliness with contentment' is 'great gain'? Or that the materialism of this age can be 'a snare'?[22]

But then it is just as possible for us to come to the Bible with reservations about the supernatural. We have been reared to think in that way. Our generation has sanctified doubt. When I first learned in Sunday school about the miracles, it was with the rider that 'God does not do things like that nowadays'. No wonder we get such a shock when he does!

Ironically, the spiritual vacuum which this has created has left us open to a pop existentialism which encourages us to live by the tides of emotion and to trim our attitude to God's Word by the feelings of the day. We have to 'feel led' before we get on and do anything. We talk about our 'experiences' – by which we mean how we felt at the time – and our 'problems' – by which we mean times when we do not feel so good. It really has little to do with being a Christian. It is simply the spirit of the age in which we live.

We can never finally free ourselves from this kind of thing, but we can try to bring our attitudes under the judgment of the Word of God. The world view which we assume to be the only one may be far removed from the way in which God wants Christians to think. We need the grace — and the courage — to go to Scripture and face its teaching squarely instead of explaining it away. We need men and women who will dare to put themselves *under* the Word of God once again.

Notes

1. J. B. Phillips, *The Ring of Truth* (Hodder and Stoughton, 1967), p. 18.

2. See L. Morris, *I Believe in Revelation* (Hodder and Stoughton, 1976); C. Pinnock, *Biblical Revelation* (Moody, 1971).

3. For example: Mt. 4:4, 7, 10; Mk. 12:35–37; Lk. 4:16–21; Jn. 10:34–36; *etc*.

4. See detailed discussion in J. W. Wenham, *Christ and the Bible* (IVP, 1972).

5. For example; 1 Cor. 14:37; 1 Thes. 2:13; 1 Pet. 1:23–25; 1 Jn. 4:6; *etc*.

6. 2 Pet. 3:15–16.

7. A. C. Thiselton, in I. H. Marshall (ed.), *New Testament Interpretation* (Paternoster, 1977), p. 114.

8. Rom. 1:3–4.

9. For example, 1 Pet. 1:10–12.

10. Gal. 4:8–9.

11. C. F. Evans, *Is 'Holy Scripture' Christian?* (SCM, 1971), p. 34.

12. 1 Cor. 15:11.

13. For example, Gal. 1:6–9.

14. 1 Cor. 15:29.

15. Mt. 27:3–10; *cf*. Acts 1:18–19.

16. S. T. Davis, *The Debate about the Bible* (Westminster, 1977).

17. H. Lindsell, *The Battle for the Bible* (Zondervan, 1976), p. 18.

18. R. T. France, 'Inerrancy and New Testament Exegesis', in *Themelios* 1.1, Autumn 1975, p. 16.

19. In I. H. Marshall (ed.), *New Testament Interpretation*, p. 134.

20. Rom. 3:4.

21. 'Hermeneutics and Biblical Authority', in *Themelios* 1.1. Autumn 1975, p. 6.

22. 1 Tim. 6:6–10.

God still speaks: How to hear him in Scripture

JOHN WHITE

THEY seemed an unlikely bunch. I was sure they were *bona fide* Christians. I had led them to Christ myself. Yet just as I would be feeling reassured that they were turning out well, they would do and say the strangest things. I clucked over them like a nervous hen worried lest I had hatched swans.

We were all students in the same residence hall. Somehow they did not conform to my stereotype of a Christian. Not that conforming to a stereotype was important, but they just didn't seem to be 'tuned in.'

Yet one year later I had no hesitation in calling them godly. They knew what they believed and knew where they were going in life. They had become Christians. The only way I can account for the difference was that during the intervening months we all had been studying Scripture steadily, both individually and collectively.

Pat, a six-foot, genial athlete, was another guy who had

me worried. Friendly, helpful, but clueless. On impulse I loaned him a book about daily Bible study and never saw him again for six months.

When we ran across each other later I was astounded. Same face. Same build. Different man.

I had forgotten about the book but Pat hadn't. 'It changed my life,' he told me seriously, 'at least, daily, prayerful Bible study did.' It was not the sort of language he would have used six months before.

Pat has now been a missionary for many years. I need not have been surprised. Scripture claims to have profound effects on us. 'Like newborn babies,' writes Peter, 'crave pure spiritual milk, *so that by it you may grow up in your salvation*' (1 Pet. 2:2).

The benefits of Bible study

The very life of God was planted within you when you became a Christian. You were born again. Spiritual life, like biological life, has its own developmental needs, one of which is truth. As you absorb truth from Scripture, spiritual life will thrive within you. As Peter says, you will grow as you feed on the milk of the Word.

Scripture truth is more than milk, however. It varies in texture and substance, and correspondingly in ease of digestion. The more you develop spiritually the better able you will be to stomach the 'meat' of Scripture. Strong truth makes strong Christians stronger.

Scripture also gives you clear moral guidelines to live by. They will not always be in the form of simple 'do's and don'ts'. God designed Scripture to give moral orientation to people living in any culture, in any age and in any moral climate.

Your sense of right and wrong (call it 'conscience' or 'super-ego' or whatever) was developed by your upbringing and by other moral influences surrounding you. If you were reared by parents who were strong-minded teetotallers, you would feel uneasy if you start to drink irrespective of the real morality of drinking. People in some savage tribes kill under certain circumstances with a feeling of doing a virtuous thing. Few people in the West would feel the same way. You may even have questioned whether absolute rights and wrongs exist.

They do. God himself is the absolute standard, and while such matters as motive and local custom are of great importance, there are moral absolutes in the very structure of the universe. But how do you find them? How can consciences be reoriented?

Scripture sheds light on morality because it reveals God himself. Study it with a willingness to pay the cost of obedience, and order will gradually replace confusion. 'How can a young man keep his way pure? By living according to your word' (Ps. 119:9).

But Scripture will do more. Truth liberates. It not only reveals a standard but will set you free to keep it. This is what makes Scripture so different from other ethical systems, which are powerless to help the struggler. You may not experience Scripture's full effect at once, but as time goes on it will become increasingly influential in shaping your behaviour. 'I have hidden your word in my heart that I might not sin against you' (Ps. 119:11).

The change will not be without conflict. There is a personal devil. Habit will be on his side as he actively opposes your attempts to live as God would have you live. (I talk more about the subject in my book, *The Fight*.) The weapon most effective in countering his attacks according to St. Paul is 'the sword of the Spirit, which is the word of God' (Eph. 6:17). A knowledge of Scripture is invaluable when you encounter the power of darkness.

There are other things Scripture will do for you. It will make you wise: wiser than people around you; wiser than your lecturers. Notice, I said *wiser*, not more knowledgeable. A wise person is one who can distinguish what is fundamental from what is trivial, who knows what life is about and who acts appropriately whatever the circumstances.

In the university there are many people who can impress us with incomprehensible twaddle. There are also brilliant scholars. But there are few who are wise. 'I have more insight than all my teachers,' wrote a psalmist long ago, 'for I meditate on your statutes. I have more understanding than the elders, for I obey your precepts' (Ps. 119:99–100).

Wisdom, you must understand, is always humble and open to learn. The wisdom that God gives through Scripture does not lead you to quote a Bible verse to contradict a biology lecturer's assertions. Such actions spring from bigotry and naïveté rather than godly wisdom.

Another part of the role of Scripture is that God guides us in our Christian lives as we read it. The same psalmist already quoted wrote, 'Your word is a lamp to my feet and a light for my path' (Ps. 119:105). However, he was talking about a *moral* pathway rather than a geographic one. The Bible is not a horoscope. Never try to read into Scripture mysterious instructions about your daily activities.

Neither is the Bible a sedative. It does not tranquillize. Yet in reading it you will find peace. 'Great peace have they who love your law' (Ps. 119:165). Chemical tranquillizing agents can work by blunting the impact reality has on you. Scripture does not. It imparts peace by showing you how to resolve any inner conflicts that destroy peace.

Peace is more than the absence of anxiety. It is a positive

56

quality arising from inner harmony. A peace which is destroyed by external threats is no peace. God's peace, which will grow the more you understand Scripture, defies uncertainty and danger. It is the clear-eyed peace with which the Roman Christians faced hungry lions in ancient arenas and with which Eastern European Christians have faced imprisonment, torture and threats to their families. It is a peace which comes from the understanding that God is in charge, that you belong to him, and that chaos and uncertainty around you represent only the confusing surface of reality.

And such peace, understandably, improves your physical well-being. It is 'marrow to your bones.'

Practical problems

I could continue to list the benefits of regular Scripture reading, but why should I? The living God has spoken. The ruler of the universe has revealed himself in print. Yet still we hesitate. Why?

You may, of course, have doubts that the Bible is inspired by God. You may feel uncomfortable precisely because you are supposed to approach it with reverence or with a special set of feelings which you cannot produce because of your inner doubts.

The best way to deal with those inner doubts is to expose yourself to the Bible. Don't approach it with any special feelings, except for a willingness to put into practice any truth you see in it. I could argue about inspiration, but I refuse to. Find out for yourself. The least we can say about the Bible is that it is a compilation of historical documents whose validity (as historical data) is now above reproach. Read it and let it speak to you. Pray, 'Please show me, O

God, if these documents *do* constitute your Word.' But read openly. Try to understand what is actually being said. Be willing to incorporate whatever truth you see into your own life.

'Ah, you have me there,' a research scientist once confessed to me thoughtfully. 'I'm not sure I can take the risk. It might mean leaving my job and being a missionary or something.' He was not joking. Few people are quite so honest, and I could offer him no guarantees as to what demands might be made of him.

On the other hand your problem may be the very opposite. You may be *too* conscious of the Bible's unique character – so conscious, in fact, that you are inhibited when you read.

Many years ago in Latin America I was astonished to discover that Roman Catholic students (who in those days had had little or no exposure to Scripture) and communist students were far better at Bible study than students from evangelical churches. In group study the communists and Catholics were quick to see what the passage *actually said*. Many evangelical students, on the other hand, had a mental block at this point. They seemed only able to see what the Bible *was supposed to say*. It was as though they screened Bible statements through a doctrinal filter, seeing that which they had been trained to expect. ('It can't say *that* because the Bible doesn't teach that.')

Or maybe you expect some kind of magic. I think that was my problem some years ago. I had a preconceived notion as to *how* God would speak from Scripture. When what I expected did not take place I was confused and disappointed.

Scripture is not magic. It is truth expressed in words, sentences and paragraphs. (The verse numbers and chapter headings are artificial and were imposed by translators long after the original documents were compiled.)

But someone will object, 'Isn't it true that the Bible can only be understood when the Holy Spirit opens our understanding and speaks to us from it?' Quite so. But the question almost implies that the Holy Spirit needs to be persuaded. It seems to suggest that before he can speak, you have to go through a special 'tuning in' session or that the words themselves are difficult and obscure, so that only if you are in some specially inspired condition, can obscurity be resolved into profundity.

God's desire is to make matters plain to anyone, anytime, anywhere. In addition to providing us with documents that are for the most part simply and clearly written, he quickens our minds by his Spirit, provided we genuinely want to know. Pride, prejudice and preconceptions are the big barriers to seeing truth. Be humble. Look at what is there. Tell God you know your mind has limitations. Thank him that he will help you understand.

Of course we use the word 'understand' in two ways. Sometimes when we say, 'I don't understand,' we mean, 'I can't grasp what the writer is trying to say.' At other times we mean, 'I can see what he's saying all right, but I don't see how it could be true.'

Both types of problem can arise when you read Scripture. The problem of the words not making sense often resolves itself when you use a modern translation. The second kind of problem ('I see what it says, but I can't believe it's true') is a sign that you are thinking about what you are reading. People who never hit problems of this sort are only going through the motions of reading.

The first thing to do is to make sure you *have* read the passage correctly. You may be puzzling over something it didn't say in the first place. But if having checked you are still shaking your head, there are many steps you can take.

You are not likely to be the first person to be puzzled. Chances are that many people have already wrestled with the same problem. Some of their thoughts will be recorded in Bible commentaries. (We'll talk about these later.) You may be puzzled simply because the Scripture conflicts with your prior ideas about what the Bible *ought* to say. But in any case, remember that in learning about the most profound mysteries of being, you are likely to come across ideas that shake and disturb you. Some will be gateways to profound insights. Others will continue to puzzle you. If they do, don't stop learning, but file the puzzle in the 'unsolved' compartment of your mind, having committed the matter to God in prayer. Five years from now you may not understand what it was that bothered you.

How to study

There are several ways to study the Bible. I hope you will eventually use all of them, but to start with one or two will be sufficient. None of the methods can be divided rigidly from any other. Their boundaries overlap. Each, when used properly, tends to check the weaknesses of the others.

You can study the Bible devotionally

By this I mean that during the regular time of quiet you spend with God each day, you can meditate prayerfully on a few verses of Scripture. Whatever other form of study you adopt, do adopt this one.

It is best to follow some regular plan (like *Meeting with God* or *Scripture Union Notes*). Devotional reading does not mean you must switch your intellect off. It simply means your emphasis should be that of a personal application, in a spirit of reverence, of what you read.

I had my own little scheme years ago. In a pocket notebook I would make a quick note of whatever helpful lesson arose from the passage. In the margin of my Bible I would jot down the reference next to the verse that had spoken to me. 'B65' would mean that my comment on the verse could be found in notebook B, page 65. As I went through the Bible several times some verses would have several references beside them, as fresh insights came. Having to jot something down kept me on my toes and helped me avoid mental laziness. It also forced me to clarify hazy insights.

Devotional Bible study is helpful if there are questions in your mind as you read, such as:

- Is there a warning for me here?
- Is there a promise I can claim?
- Are there commands I must obey?
- Is there a sin I must avoid or confess?
- Is there some encouragement I can take to heart?
- Is there some new lesson about God I can thank him for?
- Are there words of praise I can echo?
- Is there an experience described that has been true of me?

The disadvantage of confining Bible study to devotional study is that it offers an unbalanced diet — too much milk, too little meat. It needs to be supplemented by other forms.

You can study a whole book of the Bible inductively

Inductive study is the kind where you look at a whole book in an attempt to find the basic principles it demonstrates. You ask such questions as, 'What are the main points the writer is making? How can I express them in my own words?'

Inductive and deductive reasoning are complementary. You need both in any discipline. Too many students confine their approach to the Bible to a deductive one, saying 'Since A and B are true, then according to my rule the book should say X and Y.' With deductive reasoning you begin with a rule, and test the material by your rule. Inductive reasoning on the other hand looks at the material to try to find *what rules arise from it*. As both kinds of reasoning have been used in understanding the Scripture, Bible students have been amazed at the unity and consistency of its teaching. But beginners should start with an inductive approach.

Inductive Bible study lays the groundwork for systematic study. It can be carried out alone or with a group of people who agree to study the same book and who can check one another's thinking. Many books have been written to teach you the principles of this kind of study. See the Further Reading list on page 159.

I have very strong feelings about inductive Bible study and I plan to amplify them at the end. Skip anything you like in this chapter, but do read the last few pages.

You can also read the Bible through from beginning to end

This is a less formidable task than you might suppose. G. Campbell Morgan once read the whole Bible through aloud and at pulpit speed in 96 hours. If you read four chapters a day you will cover the material in about nine months.

There are advantages in this sort of reading. You get a 'bird's eye' view of a wide variety of biblical writings over a period of 1600 years. You also pick up the astonishing interrelatedness of the various parts of Scripture — particularly of the Old and New Testaments. Many of the passages will become treasures as you discover them yourself for the first time. Other passages you may have to wade through.

Use a modern translation for this sort of reading. Try it as a bedtime snack.

You can also study the Bible systematically or doctrinally

By this I mean you trace a given idea through the whole Bible. You might also want to compare what you find with what scholars down the ages have written.

This is by far the toughest form of study, and to my way of thinking it should not be tackled until one has a mastery of the other three methods (though many Bible teachers begin by instructing new converts in this method).

Again, there are a number of books which are helps in beginning this type of study, and I mention them also at the end of the chapter.

The time factor

'How can I find time to do all this Bible study? Christ promised to give me rest, yet it seems all he does is to load me with extra assignments.'

Not really. It is not Christ who overloads us with assignments. We overload ourselves. We perpetually take on more than we can do, then complain we are overworked. Among the things we load ourselves with are some that are good but not essential and many that are trivial and meaningless. Life becomes simpler when we wise up to the fact that we do not need to busy ourselves with two-thirds of our daily activities. Life stripped to its essentials is freedom.

And for the Christian, serious Bible study is an essential.

Get rid of some non-essentials in your life and set aside a regular, weekly three-hour period for serious Bible study in addition to your daily reading.

You find time to eat, to sleep, to wash and to work. Some people also find time to attend a weekly movie or to spend hours playing games, watching TV, practising hobbies, playing instruments, socializing. Find time to study the Bible whatever else you may have to drop.

But how do I proceed? Let's say I free up three hours a week to study the Bible. What do I do then?

First you make sure that you have proper study materials. To start you will need:

● A modern translation of the Bible (or New Testament)
● A looseleaf notebook.

In addition it will be helpful to buy one or both of the following:

● *The New Bible Commentary Revised*
● *The New Bible Dictionary*.

Where shall I begin to study? You must decide on a book to study. If you are a new Christian, I suggest that you start with Luke's Gospel. I feel that to start with *one* of the four Gospels is a must. The Gospel of John was written to convince non-Christians of Christ's deity. For that reason, while it may be good to study John, my suggestion would be to begin with one of the other three.

Each of these three Gospels has points in its favour. The value of all of them is that they serve to emphasize Christianity as an historical faith. It stands or falls on events that took place in time and space. Supremely it is centred in the life, teachings, death and resurrection of the God-man who entered time-space via the uterus of a peasant woman two thousand years ago.

Luke's Gospel, more than any other, is preoccupied with the problem of sifting and analysing all the reports surrounding the birth, life, death and resurrection of Jesus, and with recording as accurate an account of them as possible. For this reason I recommend it as a starting point for your serious study. But if you have other convictions about other books in the Bible which you want to get at first, please remember I am only suggesting.

Having collected my notebook, Bible and my commentaries, how do I proceed? Well, if you're a serious student in other subjects, I really shouldn't have to tell you. While no real understanding of Scripture is possible apart from the Holy Spirit, the *techniques* of Bible study differ from no other textual study. But to refocus your thinking, let me remind you that your object in any textual study is:

1. to see exactly what the text says,
2. to decide what the text means, and
3. to explore the relevance of the text to contemporary life generally and to your own life in particular.

This being so you must understand the contexts. First, you must understand the context of the whole book. By reading either the introduction to the book in the *New Bible Commentary Revised* or the relevant entry in the *New Bible Dictionary* you will learn something about the time the book was written, contemporary concerns and problems. something about the authorship, plus problems and discussions that have preoccupied previous students of the book. But only read the detailed analysis of the book in the commentary *after* your personal study of the text.

You should write brief notes from your reading to summarize what you see as important from this to clarify your grasp of the *contextual climate* surrounding the whole book.

Then you should read right through the book — not just once, but several times. Don't read with a blank mind. Read probing for answers to questions. What is the writer's purpose in writing? Why does he record the incidents he does? Is there any plan to the book, or is it written haphazardly? Can it be divided into sections, and if so can titles be given to the sections? Are there any themes running through the book from beginning to end, like a *leitmotif* in a piece of music?

When you are able to answer these questions add a further introductory section to your notes. Try at the same time to write down a very simple outline of what *you* see as its main sections and where they begin and end.

You will then be in a position to examine each section in detail for you will have begun to understand the general context in which each paragraph, each sentence, each word is found. And as you do so you will keep in mind the same three basic questions: What does the passage actually say? What does it mean? How does it apply here and now? Never tackle the third question before you have answered the second. Discipline yourself fiercely never to answer the second question until you have looked the first one squarely in the face.

I need say no more for now. Many, many helpful books have been written on this whole subject. I only wish to let a wild, warm enthusiasm flow from my heart down my arm to flood from my pen on to the paper. Bible study has torn apart my life and remade it. That is to say that God, through his Word, has done so. In the darkest periods of my life when everything seemed hopeless, I would struggle in the grey dawns of many faraway countries to grasp the basic truths of Scripture passages. I looked for no immediate answers to my problems. Only did I sense intuitively that I was drinking draughts from a fountain that gave life to my soul.

Slowly as I grappled with textual and theological problems, a strength grew deep within me. Foundations cemented themselves to an other-worldly rock beyond the reach of time and space, and I became strong and more alive. If I could write poetry about it I would. If I could sing through paper, I would flood your soul with the glorious melodies that express what I have found. I cannot exaggerate for there are no expressions majestic enough to tell of the glory I have seen or of the wonder of finding that I, a neurotic, unstable, middle-aged man have my feet firmly planted in eternity and breathe the air of heaven. And all this has come to me through a careful study of Scripture.

Setting a goal

For in this study I have experienced an ever-deepening knowledge of a person. We talk about *knowing* but in two different senses. I can know facts. But I can also know people. Knowing facts is an intellectual process. Knowing people involves emotional and volitional interactions with them.

You may read the Bible to know certain facts. But this is only the beginning. Your real aim is to know Christ. You must therefore set yourself, as you study Scripture, to get to know a person.

There are many experts on the Bible. Some will awe you by the facility with which they quote chapter and verse. Others will hint at a knowledge of the original languages. You will come across people with a formidable fund of information on any passage you could name, ready to expatiate on the subtler nuances of the biblical text at the drop of a hat.

Don't mimic them.

Knowledge, especially biblical knowledge, has the same effect as wine when it goes to your head. You become dizzily exalted. But Bible study should be conducted not with a view to *knowing about* Christ but to *knowing him* personally.

And to know Christ is to know peace. The more you know him, the less inclined you will be to impress people or to indulge in games of biblical one-upmanship. The Bible was inspired because God wants you to know him. He wants to reveal his heart to you in a love relationship. If you let him, he will make that relationship so precious that it will become a private thing that you will want to share with no-one. You may be willing enough to talk about him. You will be glad to tell others of his goodness. But there will be secret issues that are between you and him alone. And he will make your life as stable as a rock and as alive as spring.

> Beyond the sacred page
> I seek Thee, Lord,
> My spirit pants for Thee,
> O living Word.

A few suggestions

A. Aids to Bible study.

1. *The New Bible Commentary Revised*: A one-volume commentary. Helpful provided you try to get to grips with the passage *before* you examine the commentary's analysis of the biblical text itself.

2. *The New Bible Dictionary*: A superb tool for Bible study − really an encyclopaedia on any topic in the Bible. Included are entries giving background on every book in the Bible.

3. *Search the Scriptures*: A handy three-year course. It prevents you from falling into haphazard daydreaming by asking penetrating questions, and gives notes on tough

verses. It takes you through the entire Bible.

4. *Scripture Union Notes*: There is a broad range from serious notes for advanced study to simple devotional ones for young Christians. All have the same basic aim — to encourage profitable daily Bible study.

B. For your own 'Quiet Time'.

1. Read Psalm 19. As you read, make a note of the two ways in which God has revealed himself to human beings.

2. Verses 1—6. It is sometimes suggested that it is impossible to know anything about God apart from Scripture. What can be known from celestial bodies, and who can know it?

3. Verses 7—10. The words *law, testimony, statutes* and so forth are all used synonymously here. Make a list of what they can do for you.

4. Verses 11—14. Try repeating these verses aloud and making them your own prayer.

CHAPTER FOUR

What does the Bible say?

JOHN BALCHIN

WHAT about Genesis chapter one? Did God create the world in six twenty-four-hour days, or did he use evolution as his method over long and indefinite periods of time? Those who take the former line argue from the 'evening and morning' phrases; those who take the latter from the fact that 'day' does not always mean twenty-four hours in the Old Testament. But this is surely all beside the point when we ask what the original *intention* of this chapter was. What are we meant to learn here? Just this, that there is a God who created with infinite ease; that his creation was good; that human beings, who were the apex of that creation, were different in kind from the rest. The passage actually tells us nothing about God's *method*. It probably never occurred to the author to ask that kind of question. He *intended* other things.

What did they want to say?

As we consider the question 'What does the Bible say?', we

need to ask about the *intention* of the biblical writers. 'What did the author mean when he first penned this?' 'How would the first readers have understood it?' Our first job is to try to get into the shoes of the original parties and see it from their point of view. In this chapter we are going to look at what we need to know if we are going to do just that, but before we get down to the nuts and bolts, there is a matter we have to clear up before we can move on.

Intentions

The question 'What did the author intend?' is no longer as straightforward as it might seem. It has been the fashion for some years now in literary circles to talk about the author's intentions in terms of what motivated him, the personal experiences or circumstances or even state of mind which made him write as he did. If we read between the lines we are supposed to be able to discover these things.

This psychological approach to literature can almost become a form of allegorizing itself. We are told that we must not simply enjoy or appreciate the tale being told, but rather look beneath the surface for the personal implications. Hence *Alice in Wonderland* should tell us more about the Rev. Charles Dodgson's Victorian inhibitions than about Alice, and so on.

As always happens, there has been a strong reaction to all this. It has been recognized that too much literary and artistic criticism arises from *the imagination of the critic*! It is often highly questionable if the motives attributed to the author ever existed in his unattainable unconscious mind. There must be literary works where the author has no intention of revealing why he was writing, just as one can conceive of other occasions when authors were blissfully unaware of what made them write as they did. Again, there have been situations when the product has been certainly very different from the author's stated intentions.[1]

We have seen a similar movement among biblical scholars whose theories as to the origins, situations and structure of the Bible books have, at times, become unbelievably subtle. It ought to be warning enough that a good number of these hypotheses, some of which have dominated the world of biblical scholarship for a while, have fallen apart as fresh evidence has come to light, or simply as the fashion has passed. One suspects that a good deal of biblical criticism tells us more about the critic's mind, not to say his imagination, than it does about the authors of Scripture and what they intended. We need not be for ever hunting up complicated motives behind the writing of Bible books.

What sort of book?

How much we can actually know about a particular author's state of mind will depend largely upon the type of writing we have before us. A highly personal, confessional letter such as 2 Corinthians is going to reveal much more to us about Paul than, say, 2 Chronicles is about its author, whoever he was. Although every historian has his reasons for writing (and that would include, for example, the authors of the gospels), something a good number of modern scholars cannot come to terms with is the fact that an author might be narrating an account simply for its own sake and not for some abstruse theological reason. As D. M. Baillie once said of the gospel critics, 'It seldom seems to occur to them that the story may have been handed on simply or primarily *because it was true*.'[2] One of the reasons for this is the deep, one might almost say pathological, scepticism with which some scholars approach the material.[3]

Written by people

To say that the Bible is literature has sometimes been to put conservative evangelicals on red alert for heresy! 'Surely', would come the rejoinder, 'the Bible is inspired', and inspired in a different sense from other so-called 'inspired' literature. (And they would probably quote 2 Timothy 3:16 into the bargain!)

A human book

All this is true — the Bible authors often claim as much themselves, as we shall see later. But at the same time, whatever the mystery and miracle of inspiration involved, the Bible did not drop from heaven on golden plates, nor was it dictated in some sort of heavenly typing-pool. Biblical inspiration means that God took up and involved the full humanity of the Bible authors as well as giving us a great deal more. So, in Paul's writings we *do* meet with Paul, and in Jeremiah's prophecy we come face to face with the prophet himself. God used real people with individual personalities which came across in their writings. Scripture is *both human and divine*, and if we are to understand it properly we must come to terms with both these aspects. Unfortunately in recent years, while conservatives have stressed the latter, modernists have concentrated on the former. Both positions are unbalanced.

We shall be looking at the Bible from the divine point of view later on. Concentrating for a while on the human side, we have to regard the Bible as a collection of writings in human language coming out from a human background, that is, as literature.

Literary styles

What is more, literature can be diverse in its expression, and the biblical collection is a good example of this. We not only have *narrative prose* (*e.g.* the gospels); we also have *personal letters* (*e.g.* those of Peter, John and Paul), we have *legal documents* (*e.g.* Leviticus) and we have large tracts of *poetry* (*e.g.* the Psalms) — to mention just a few of the different styles. Each of these will demand a different approach.

For example, in poetry there is a licence of expression and an employment of idiom which it would be fatal to understand in wooden, literal terms. (You try it with 'I wandered lonely as a cloud . . .' and see where it gets you!) This has now long been recognized to the point where most modern translations will attempt to print biblical poetry as poetry and not, as the Authorized Version did, in solid chunks of prose.

Fact not fiction

Let's not be guilty of making the mental equation: 'Literature equals fiction.' Some have argued this way, bracketing the Bible with other classic pieces of literature, good for us (like Shakespeare) because they form part of our cultural heritage. Just as we recognize Hamlet and King Lear as imaginary figures, and think no less of them because of that, we must approach Abraham or David or Paul in the same way, they say. It is true, of course, that the Bible has an undisputed place in western culture, but to say that the Bible is literature is not to say that it is not true or historical or that its characters never existed. It can contain fictional elements (for example, Jesus' parables are fiction) but it is literature in that it was written to be read.

A long time ago

A further complication when it comes to understanding

biblical style is that its phraseology and diction are not what we are used to. The Bible is not only literature; it is ancient literature, with some parts more ancient than others. In fact, it would be better to talk about biblical *styles*, remembering that the earliest and latest biblical books were composed hundreds of years apart and in very different circumstances, not to say languages.

Different language

It is for this reason that it is very difficult to get an 'accurate' modern translation. In order to put the Bible into language which the modern man in the street can understand, the translator has to paraphrase, thereby inevitably, to some degree, losing touch with the original texts. This is why a good 'study' translation might not be the easiest to read.

For example, the Good News Bible, or even a version as racy as the Living Bible, comes over to us in ordinary, everyday language. This is not a bad thing. After all, the originals would have been in the everyday language of their own day. But they do this by paraphrasing to a greater or lesser degree the Greek, Hebrew and Aramaic in which the Bible was first written. That means that their translators have tried to find modern equivalents for phrases and statements in the old languages. For example, those who (literally) 'hunger and thirst for righteousness' become 'those whose greatest desire is to do what God requires' in the Good News Bible.[4] This reasonably represents the *ideas* in the text, if not the actual words. It is a different matter when the American edition of the Living Bible tells us that 'Saul went into the cave to go to the bathroom'![5] To get a little nearer to what the Bible actually said we need to go to something like the Revised Standard Version or the New International

Version. The phrasing might seem more old-fashioned to the ordinary reader, but it often represents the original words more accurately.

Different thinking

This leads us to another shattering discovery. The Bible authors did not just speak and write in languages different from ours; they *thought* differently from us. Every generation tends to ask different questions framed largely by the current philosophical outlook, the mental scaffolding in which they live and think. For example, there would be no question in those days about the supernatural dimensions to life. Everyone with very few exceptions believed in some sort of God or spiritual power, even if only superstitiously.

We must be aware of this when we come to the Bible. There must be what has been called 'historical distancing' between ourselves and such people as Isaiah and Luke, or we shall think about them as twentieth-century people.[6] Hollywood has not helped here. It becomes too easy to imagine Moses or Samson speaking with an American drawl! What is worse, if we are not careful we find ourselves reading our ways of thinking into Bible statements (Genesis 1 is a good example!), and expecting Bible authors to answer questions they never thought of asking.

We may also be tempted to think with the intellectual snobbery of the twentieth century, and look down on all things ancient as being unsophisticated and naïve. This despising of what is ancient or old in preference for what is new or young is a fairly recent idea. I have a friend who is always raving about the latest book or theory. I have often wondered just how we managed to live before it came out!

People of their time

Something that we have to remember is that we are, everyone of us, children of our own time. Our standards, values and attitudes, in fact many of the ideas we take for granted, are largely the product of the culture in which we were born. If we are unaware of this, it will mean that all our thinking about the Bible will be distorted. We shall be reading it through twentieth-century spectacles.

Different culture

But the Bible authors were not twentieth-century Christians. Far from it. They lived in times and cultures very different from our own. At the same time these historical settings are not entirely beyond our reach. Historical studies can do a great deal to reconstruct for us the ways in which men and women lived and thought then. This in turn will help us to understand better both what and why they wrote.

It is this sort of background knowledge which throws a flood of light on, for example, Paul's instructions about women and their head-covering. [7] Although there are several difficulties in that passage, it has been argued that, far from being a sign of dutiful submission to the males, it was a mark of the woman's dignity and freedom as a Christian. In a situation where loose hair might mean loose morals, Paul is appealing for propriety or decent behaviour by the standards of the day. Otherwise the fellowship would get a bad name locally. Hats mean something entirely different today, and probably have more to do with the wife's control of the household budget than with submission! Some have suggested that a modern parallel might be the custom of wearing wedding-rings. The wife's ring protects her from improper approaches, and marks her out as a married woman.

Archaeology

In this respect we are heavily in debt to that whole battery of scholars who have pursued biblical historical research. For example, biblical archaeology has opened up the world of the Bible for us, and has often cleared up difficulties in the meaning of the text. Some (*e.g.* Sir William Ramsay, who did pioneer work on the background of the book of Acts) have even convinced themselves of the accuracy of the New Testament evidence in this way. When he began his work Ramsay was very sceptical, but after he had actually examined the evidence he concluded that Luke was a painstaking and accurate historian.[8] For instance, his local knowledge of even the different titles of town officials was confirmed by inscriptions which Ramsay unearthed.

Contemporary writings

Comparative studies, where the Bible is placed alongside other ancient traditions, have also been a great help. Whereas Bible authors may come close to very different conclusions from their pagan contemporaries, we must remember that they lived in the same world and used the same stock of ideas. This is why it is legitimate to turn to non-biblical writings of the same period as, for example, the New Testament books, in order to see how people thought in those days. We have a great deal of literature from the period between the Testaments, including the Apocrypha, which brings us up to date on the ways in which the Jews of Jesus' day had developed and had been influenced in their beliefs.

New revelation

We are not saying, however, that the New Testament is just another phase of this development. The writers were certainly not confined to their background, and they often transformed the ideas they inherited under what we believe to be the creative guidance of the Holy Spirit. But though they built their house to a different plan, they used the same bricks.

The effect of the discovery of the Dead Sea Scrolls is a good illustration of this. Whereas most scholars would agree that there is no direct link between them and the biblical writings, they use many of the same terms, phrases and ideas, which in turn help us to understand the ways that they are being used in the Bible. In particular these studies have made possible a completely different approach to John's gospel, which was long considered by many to be late and unreliable. The evidence of the Scrolls points the other way. The date could be early and the account is firmly rooted in eyewitness evidence. [9]

Help for us today

It is in ways like these that historical studies have often endorsed the reliability of the biblical account or undermined theories discrediting Scripture. In the final analysis, of course, the only way to 'prove' the truth of the Bible is to live it, but in that such research has been an aid to faith, it has been highly valuable.

Fortunately, a good deal of this material is available to English readers in a variety of Bible handbooks, comment-aries and encyclopaedias. This means that the ordinary Christian can build up a background knowledge of the Bible for himself. It is possible, of course, to derive a great deal of help and comfort from God's Word without it. The Holy Spirit makes Christ and the gospel known regularly to many who have no Bible background at all. If we are going to go further than the biblical ABC, however, and intend really to get a grasp of what the Bible teaches, there can be no short cuts. In this area, like all the others, there is no royal road to learning.

A book full of pictures

There have always been Christians who have seen hidden or 'spiritual' meanings in Scripture which the authors never intended. But this mistake does touch upon a truth. This is the fact that religious language is made up of ordinary terms used in a special way.

Human models

Thomas Aquinas recognized this years ago when he taught that when we speak about God we use *analogies*. We are really trying to express the inexpressible, for God and his ways are far beyond us and what we can put into words. So, taking some human model, we say that God is like this – but then again, he is different.

For example, when we use the term 'Father' of God we arc using it in this way. There is much about the best of human fatherhood which we can credit to God, and yet even the best falls far short of his relationship with us. So we qualify the statement. We call him 'heavenly Father'.

(Sometimes, of course, this can cause problems for other reasons. I know a young girl who had great difficulty in getting hold of this particular truth because she came from a broken home where her father had been a brute to her. She had to learn what fatherhood was, seeing it demonstrated in Christian families she knew, before she could call God 'Father' with the love and confidence which that word carries for most of us.)

The Bible is rich in this sort of expression. Jesus called himself 'the Good Shepherd'; John the Baptist called him 'the

Lamb of God'. In neither case do we think of him as a *literal* shepherd or lamb, although as they come in Scripture both these terms are full of meaning. [10] For this is the language of symbol where spiritual truths are expressed in pictures. 'The Good Shepherd' speaks to me of care, protection, guidance, nurture, discipline, and much else. The 'Lamb of God' sums up ideas such as innocence and sacrifice, sin and atonement, God's provision and mankind's need.

Apocalyptic

There is one biblical style which is almost deliberate analogy and symbol from beginning to end. This is the strange (to us) picture language of 'apocalyptic', the style in which the book of Revelation is written. Images drawn from Israel's history become symbols of spiritual truths, clear and inspiring to those steeped in the Old Testament, although something of a riddle to others. It might have been originally a sort of code language used to hide holy things from unbelievers in times of persecution. [11]

It would be perilous to understand it literally, although many have fallen into that trap. One bestselling author tells us confidently that 'the kings of the East' must mean Red China; that the nightmarish cavalry described for us in the book are nothing less than helicopter gun ships; that the sealing of God's people tells us that 144,000 literal, physical, Jewish Billy Grahams will be turned loose on the earth after the church has been taken away. This kind of thing makes fascinating science-fiction reading, but it has little to do with what the book of Revelation is saying.

Real pictures

One school of thought argues that symbols and images are the clue to our understanding the Bible as a whole. The human being, it is said, thinks about 'his own being, his

81

world, his destiny and the objects of his worship' in terms of 'archetypal images', that is, pictures which answer to universal spiritual needs.[12] Most religions use pictures such as light and darkness, life and birth, death and resurrection, and the Bible is full of this kind of thing. So, they say, the inspiration of the Bible was not a matter of God passing on certain facts about himself, but rather giving the authors a series of symbols which express who God is and what he is doing. When we read the Bible, we recognize these and respond to them.[13]

This may seem a bit complicated, but there is some truth in it. The appeal of some Scripture passages is more poetic than propositional, and yet that is certainly not the whole story. The Bible does give us stated facts about God and mankind and Christ and so on which we can think about and grasp with our minds. It *is* possible to say 'what the Bible teaches . . .' It is not just a matter of 'reality apprehended by the imagination', even though God's reality might be so big that it can be expressed only in symbolic ways and by analogies.

Furthermore, although religious language must necessarily be the language of analogy, the Bible claims that what it expresses actually happened in space-time, whether it was the Exodus or the resurrection or what have you. Symbol maybe; but not fantasy fiction.

But I don't speak Greek!

The starting-point for all interpretation is naturally to come to terms with the basic material to be interpreted. With modern literature we often have the immense advantage of being in direct touch with both the language in which it is written, and with the original text of the work in question. Not so with the Bible. The Bible authors wrote in three different archaic languages — Hebrew, Aramaic and Greek — and without exception, we do not have the original texts of what they wrote, only copies of copies of copies.

Bible languages

These may appear to be insurmountable problems, but in practice this is not necessarily so. As far as the languages are concerned, we are better placed now than at any other time in history since those early days due to the long and painstaking efforts of scholars in this field. Although there are still tantalizing gaps in our knowledge, we have more understanding of the use of the words and phrases, and of the structure of those languages, than ever before.

A great deal of our insight derives from the fact that a large amount of non-biblical literature in those languages has come to light over the years which illustrates the use of biblical terms in different settings. For example, biblical scholars of the last century were restricted in their understanding of New Testament Greek, because all they had by way of comparison were classical Greek works. Since then an enormous store of literature, including books, bills and private letters, written in the same style as the New Testament, has been found. This, of course, has made some of the older scholars' conclusions out of date, but it has forwarded our current knowledge of what the Bible authors were actually trying to say.

Manuscripts

A similar thing might be said about the text of the Bible books. Here we have an embarrassment of riches. It may surprise some to learn that some of the ancient classical works are known to us by only a single, sometimes mutilated, copy. When it comes to the Bible, however, we have literally hundreds of copies as well as early translations into other languages. These latter put us in touch, at second hand, with even earlier editions. The discovery of early manuscripts over the last hundred years or so is an exciting story, and it is going on all the time. For example, when the collection of the writings of the Dead Sea Sect came to light in the 1940s, our knowledge of the Hebrew text of the Old Testament was pushed back about a thousand years nearer to the original almost overnight. (One of the remarkable aspects of these particular discoveries was that some of the Hebrew texts which turned up differed very little from modern editions which we were using.)

Copying problems

When work is copied by hand, as most of us know from personal experience, errors can creep in quite easily. The Bible texts that we have are the result of hundreds of years of copying by a variety of different hands, some careful and some not quite so careful. This has led to a large number of variant readings in the copies we have in our possession, although let us be quick to add that, as far as the bulk of the Bible is concerned, there is substantial agreement. In the early days of 'textual criticism' (as the study of these variants is called), scholars often worked by 'feel', accepting one manuscript as being fairly accurate and adjusting other readings to fit.

In recent years the study has become much more of a science and, by comparison and collection, what was the original can be established with a fair degree of probability. As with the languages, there are still gaps in our knowledge where different scholars fill in the blank or confused spaces in different ways, but none of these seriously affects the main stream of biblical truth.

Into English

The average Bible student will come to the job by way of translation, not knowing any or enough of the original languages to study at that level. Once again we have plenty of help as the last few years have seen a spate of modern translations in English. These may all be regarded as 'exegetical tools', that is, they can help us to understand what the Bible actually says. Many have had the happy experience of seeing the Bible come alive for them simply by reading the Scriptures in contemporary English. Passages obscured by out-of-date expressions in the older versions, or glossed over because we are so familiar with them, sometimes come across in a fresh light. It is useful to compare translation with translation as the odd turn of phrase or emphasis may bring out the meaning of the text for us in a way we had not grasped before.

Alistair, a young science undergraduate, came to see me one day. He was deeply depressed and was convinced that, although he thought he had become a Christian many years before, he had not been genuinely born again.

'There,' he told me, 'John says that "No-one born of God commits sin".[14] I sin, so I can't be a Christian after all.'

Of course, had he put that verse in the setting of the whole letter, he would have seen that John recognizes that Christians sin, and gives us tremendous reassurance that God will forgive.[15] So it could not mean what he thought. The clue here, however, is the original tense of the verb. John most probably meant that anyone who is really converted does not go on *habitually, repeatedly* sinning. If he lives like that, there is obviously no difference between him and an unbeliever. It was a pity that this incident happened before the New International Version came out. There it reads, 'No-one who is born of God will continue to sin.'

Get that text into context!

A text taken out of context, or so my teachers told me, often becomes a pretext. We have already seen that the weakness of 'proof-text' theology is that it can quite easily bend the original meaning of the passages. I know one good man who was fond of quoting in prayer meetings a verse which, in context, meant the exact opposite of what *he* did! And then there is that beautiful one in Isaiah often used to stimulate fellowship: 'Every one helps his neighbour, and says to his brother, "Take courage!" '[16] A great text, but the only problem is that the speakers are idolaters encouraging one another to trust in their gods! Or what about those choruses and songs addressed to Christ as 'the rose of Sharon' and 'the lily of the valley'? Has it never occurred to anyone that, in the love-song from which they were taken, it is the girl protesting that, compared with the other women at court, she was as commonplace and as ordinary as a daisy in the field?[17]

It is by taking texts out of context that you can quite easily make the Bible contradict itself. This is what Bill and Jane did.

'Why shouldn't I go down to the pub with my friends?' said Bill. 'After all, Paul said, "By all means save some." How can I witness to them if I don't have a drink with them?'

'But can't you see,' protested Jane, 'the Bible says, "Come out from them, and be separate from them"? You're just compromising the gospel by what you're doing.'

And so they hammered on for most of the evening. But who was right? After all, they both had a Bible verse to support their arguments. The two of them had taken their proof texts out of their original settings. Bill's verse, 'By all means save some', does not really justify his drinking habits. In context, Paul is speaking about giving up his rights and privileges in order to win others for Christ. [18] Whereas he does tell us that he was prepared to identify with people of cultures different from his own in order to do this, he is very careful to underline his responsibility to Christ when it came to his behaviour. What is more, when we look at the whole drift of his argument, he has some sharp things to say to those at Corinth who were compromising the gospel by their 'spiritual liberty'. [19]

At the same time, Jane was doing a similar thing with her verse. [20] The call to be separate from the world is quite clear, but we know from other things that Paul said that we should not cut ourselves off completely from our non-Christian friends. [21] Being a Christian does not mean living in a monastery!

The passage

All this adds up to the importance of the setting of a biblical statement. A verse taken from the Bible was originally part of a passage, sometimes a small section of an argument or description. Whereas some can stand on their own perfectly well without any distortion, a good number change in meaning – some slightly, some greatly – when taken out of that original setting. If we want to understand what a particular biblical statement means, we may have to ask what the whole book means if we are going to be fair to the author. Certainly we will closely study the passage in which it is found.

The words

A similar difficulty can arise from the wrong use of biblical words. It is sometimes assumed that every time a word occurs in Scripture, it must have the same meaning. An added problem is that words develop and change in their meaning over the years. In the scholarly world it had long been standard practice to trace the history of a term, seeking the way in which it had been used in and out of the Bible, and then to read that total meaning into a particular occurrence. We see a similar trend in some of our amplified translations.

In recent times, however, the absurdity of this practice has been pointed out.[22] What is important when understanding a passage is not what the word might have meant in earlier works, but how the author is actually using it there. The same words might mean different things in different settings. For example, Paul and James appear to be using the term 'faith' in almost contradictory ways. For James it means acknowledging facts about God; for Paul, it is often total commitment to God, practically 'obedience'.[23]

This does not mean that words mean nothing. They do have a stable core of meaning, but if we stop and think a moment, we never use them except in sentences or phrases where they are related to others which modify that meaning.

The ideas

Modern linguistic studies have thrown light on our use and abuse of biblical terms. From a linguistic point of view, a word is a written or spoken sound plus an idea or ideas to be conveyed by it. The sounds, of course, change with every different language. The ideas, however, may be related to others sometimes represented by different sounds. Traditional biblical word-studies have concentrated on words of the same sound, form or root, and have often missed the fact that the ideas they convey might be related to those represented by other words. So in our word-studies we should be looking for clusters of similar ideas — maybe represented by different terms — but which fill out and relate the meaning of a particular word in its context.[24]

Take a word like 'spirit' in the New Testament. In the original it can simply mean 'wind', and there are several words for that in Scripture. Sometimes it just means 'breath' in a physical sense. It is also often used of the human spirit along with 'soul' and in contrast with the body or the flesh. Equally it relates to terms like 'heart', 'conscience' and 'the inner man'. It can sum up the whole person. But it is also used in a different way of God's Spirit, of his activity and power, as well as of other spiritual beings: angels, demons, principalities and powers, even ghosts. So you can see, it would be wrong to think that it meant the same thing every time. In fact it would be highly misleading.

All this might sound a bit technical, but it adds up to this: the only way of finding out what a word means is to study the context, the phrase, the sentence and the passage in which it occurs. Whereas it is useful to know what a word means in other situations, the immediate questions will always be, 'What does it mean here?' or 'How is the author using it at this point?' Some of our devotional books have completely overlooked this, and have worked more by sound than by sense. That well-used little guide *Daily Light* is a good example of this. Whereas there is sometimes a genuine theme linking the daily selection of verses, in other cases the only connection is some word which all the verses have in common.

Did they always know?

So far we have been arguing for recovering the meaning of the text when it was first written. How about those occasions when a writer's words turn out to mean considerably more than he originally intended? We can see this in the way in which New Testament authors sometimes used Old Testament texts. Was the psalmist in Psalm 2 originally speaking about Christ or about the current king?[25] Did Hosea really have a vision of Mary and Joseph's escape with Jesus into Egypt and subsequent return?[26] Then again, we have those great Old Testament pictures, or 'types', which are taken up and filled out in the New Testament gospel. Just look at what Hebrews does with Old Testament priesthood and sacrifice. Were these things really in the authors' minds when they were first described? Is that what they *intended*?

Things that come true

Now it is true that, at an ordinary secular level, our words sometimes have a way of fulfilling themselves in a manner we never intended, something which lies behind the popular superstition of 'Don't say that — it might happen'. We may put this down to sheer coincidence, of course, but could it just be possible that some events actually cast their shadow before them? Certainly we have occasions in Scripture when someone unwittingly predicted far more than they intended. Caiaphas the high priest is a good example of this, and John sees the hand of God in it.[27] Conceivably, in a similar way, some of the Old Testament prophets were not *fully* aware of what they saw and said, although their words no doubt had a meaning for their own time and place.

Prophecy

We might even regard their words as a sort of divine *double entendre*, so that although they might not have grasped the fuller implications, God knew and foresaw that later generations would see them 'like a teacher committing truths to children whose full content they will not understand till later'.[28] Some do not make much of the fulfilment of prophecy these days, but in New Testament times, particularly in a Jewish setting, it was a powerful apologetic or 'proof' of the truth of the gospel. If the gospel of Matthew is an example of the way in which they 'explained and proved' that Jesus was the Christ, they were working on the assumption that God could make the Old Testament mean more than one thing.[29]

Behind the modern dislike of predictive prophecy is the assumption that it is putting the effect before the cause in a 'cause-and-effect' world. How can we know something before it happens if the event is the cause and our knowledge is the effect? In this way scholars have had to explain away the 'precognitive' element in Scripture, when the writers claim to foresee forthcoming events. But is this really necessary? We are now waking up to the fact that being aware of something before it happens is a far more common experience than has been hitherto admitted. Add the divine dimension and there is nothing improbable in the idea of God preparing the way for the gospel. In this sense, whether the prophets saw and understood or not, God was setting the scene for his Son.

Fuller meaning

To be fair, the 'fuller meaning' that New Testament authors sometimes see in Old Testament references is not really arbitrary, although it might seem that way to us. It is true that there is a difference between the historical king and his enthronement ceremony in Psalm 2 on the one hand, and the incarnation on the other. Yet at the same time there is a similarity, a line of continuity, between the two. The later truth, which the author may not have known, is closely related to the truth he did know; 'so that in hitting out at something like it, he was in touch with the very same reality in which the fuller truth is rooted.'[30]

We might add that it could be legitimate for us to use passages of Scripture in a similar way. Jesus' encounter with the woman at the well may not have been originally intended as a model of pastoral counselling, but to use the passage in this way would be entirely consistent with the original intention.[31] This is different again from allegorizing. We are suggesting an analogy where the same principles apply.

Take, for example, the story of David and Goliath. Very few of us are likely to be shepherd boys, almost certainly not on the hills of Palestine, and I would guess that none of us has had to fight a Philistine giant. Yet at the same time, there are abiding principles in what David did which are the same today as they were then. The big lesson, of course, is that of trusting God when we meet the challenges of life, and of proving God's protection and provision as we step out in faith. And we can probably think of other lessons which we can quite legitimately transfer from David's experience to our own.

We must, of course, take care that our analogy really is consistent with the original, or we will be once again falling into the trap of fanciful allegorizing. As C. S. Lewis once said in this connection, 'What we see when we think we are looking into the depths of Scripture may sometimes be only the reflection of our own silly faces.'[32]

Types

'Typology' is similar, but somewhat different too. It is not simply seeing a profounder sense in Old Testament figures and events; there is often a contrast involved as well. Christ is our heavenly king in a way no earthly king ever could be; heaven is our spiritual Jerusalem; and so on. Once again we are warned by the misuse of this line of approach to tread very carefully, or we shall be seeing 'types' and their corresponding 'antitypes' (as they are called) everywhere.

It was said of one early church theologian that he saw the cross in every stick mentioned in the Old Testament! A good rule would be to ask if the parallel is warranted by the New Testament, and to confine ourselves to what the inspired authors saw and wrote. For example, in the book of Hebrews, the Old Testament system of priests and sacrifices is seen as having its fulfilment in who Christ is and what he did. But the writer does not go into detailed parallels between the blessings of the gospel and the furniture in the tabernacle or the high priest's clothes, as some later writers have done.

In our quest for what the Bible authors originally intended and what the book actually means, we have now gone one step further. We have been assuming that we are not just dealing with an ordinary book; that God had a hand in its composition. When we see the New Testament writers using verses in a fuller sense, or claiming Old Testament types to be fulfilled, we have to allow for the sovereignty of God in the whole operation. When we deal with the writings of Scripture we are looking for the divine intention as much as for the human.

Notes

1. R. Wellek and A. Warren. *Theory of Literature* (Penguin, 1963), pp. 147–150; E. W. M. Tillyard and C. S. Lewis, *The Personal Heresy* (OUP, 1965).

2. D. M. Baillie, *God was in Christ* (Faber, 1948), p. 57.

3. For a useful discussion of this subject see C. S. Lewis, *Fern-Seeds and Elephants* (Collins, 1977), pp. 104–125.

4. Mt. 5:6.

5. 1 Sa. 24:3.

6. A. C. Thiselton in J. R. W. Stott (ed.), *Obeying Christ in a Changing World* (Collins, 1977), p. 100.

7. 1 Cor. 11:1−16.

8. I. H. Marshall in I. H. Marshall (ed.), *New Testament Interpretation* (Paternoster, 1977), pp. 126−127.

9. J. A. T. Robinson, *Twelve New Testament Studies* (SCM, 1962), pp. 94−106.

10. C. Brown, *Philosophy and the Christian Faith* (IVP, 1968), pp. 30−32.

11. L. Morris, *Apocalyptic* (IVP, 1973).

12. A. Richardson, *The Bible in an Age of Science* (SCM, 1961), pp. 142−163.

13. A. Richardson, *The Bible in the Age of Science* (SCM, 1961), p. 161.

14. 1 Jn. 3:9.

15. 1 Jn. 2:1−2.

16. Is. 41:6.

17. Song 2:1.

18. 1 Cor. 9:22.

19. 1 Cor. 10:23−33.

20. 2 Cor. 6:17.

21. 1 Cor. 5:9−10.

22. J. Barr, *The Semantics of Biblical Language* (OUP, 1961).

23. Eph. 2:8−10; Rom. 4:1−25; *cf.* Jas. 2:14−26.

24. A. C. Thiselton in I. H. Marshall (ed.), *New Testament Interpretation*, pp. 75−104.

25. Ps. 2:7; *cf.* Heb. 1:5.

26. Ho. 11:1; *cf.* Mt. 2:15.

27. Jn. 11:49−52.

28. R. E. Brown, 'The Sensus Plenior in the Last Ten Years', *Catholic Biblical Quarterly* 25.2 (July, 1963), p. 265.

29. Acts 17:3.

30. C. S. Lewis, *Reflections on the Psalms* (Bles, 1958), p. 102.

31. I. H. Marshall in I. H. Marshall (ed.), *New Testament Interpretation*, p. 14.

32. C. S. Lewis, *Reflections on the Psalms* (Bles, 1958), p. 121.

CHAPTER FIVE

Word and Spirit: The Bible and the gift of prophecy today

I. The inspiration and authority of Scripture

ROY CLEMENTS

I am an evangelical Christian. By that, I mean that I look to the Bible for an authoritative answer on all matters of my Christian faith and conduct. I am convinced that evangelical Christianity is the only kind of Christianity that can commend Christ in an adequate way to our secularized contemporary society. And, for that reason, I am passionately concerned for the maintenance of evangelical unity within the Christian church.

But I am worried about the state of evangelicalism today.

It seems to me that we are in danger of being divided by rival spiritualities. I'll call them the spirituality of the Word and the spirituality of the Spirit.

The evidences of this split are glaringly apparent. It colours both styles of worship and styles of evangelism. So acute is this division of interests becoming that it is increasingly difficult for those who belong to one camp to remain happily in a congregation made up of those who belong to the other. We feel threatened by one another, suspicious of one another, even hostile toward one another. Worst of all, we find it difficult to talk to one another. Yet both these spiritualities − 'Word' and 'Spirit' − belong in very large measure to what was once the unbroken sphere of evangelical unity.

A whole range of issues is involved in this threatened division, but one of the most important is the question of 'prophecy' in the church today. Many evangelicals, holding the view that Scripture is God's full and final word of revelation to us, feel uncomfortable with others within the evangelical fold who maintain that God speaks to us today through Spirit-given prophecy.

This chapter and the next[1] argue that both 'Word' and 'Spirit' are central to evangelicalism.

We gain our knowledge of God primarily and supremely through the Bible, which the Holy Spirit has inspired to be our infallible and sufficient guide in all matters of faith and conduct. I would maintain, however, there is a continuing gift of inspired insight available to the church through the ministry of the Holy Spirit. This gift, whilst not possessing the nature or authority of Scripture, ought to be given opportunity for its exercise within the church, if she is to know God fully as her living Head.

This chapter looks at the inspiration and authority of Scripture. The next looks at the gift of prophecy in the church today.

The central importance of the Bible

As J. I. Packer asserts in his best-selling book, Christianity is about *Knowing God*.[2] A Christian can be brave in trouble because of what he *knows* of God's sovereign providence. He can pray for forgiveness because of what he *knows* of God's love and mercy. He tries to be a better person because of what he *knows* of God's holiness. He is moved to worship because of what he *knows* of God's majesty. He evangelizes because of what he *knows* of God's salvation for the world. All Christian experience is rooted in our knowledge of God.

God is not an emotive buzz word; it is rich in cognitive content. We are able to describe the God in whom we believe. Like Jeremiah, it's our boast that we understand and know the Lord who exercises kindness, justice and righteousness on the earth (Je. 9:24). So *the* primary question for any thinking Christian must be, where do we get this treasured knowledge of God from?

Knowing God

Broadly speaking, there are two types of religious epistemology, that is, theories of knowledge. The first represents the human attempt to attain the knowledge of God by our own efforts, and that category is again sub-divided into two. On the one hand there is *rationalism* which has been very influential in the West since the Enlightenment. This seeks to discover the truth of God by the use of human reason. On the other hand there is *mysticism* which has a respected tradition within the church but is mainly characteristic of the Eastern hemisphere. This seeks the same end through the non-intellectual dimension of spiritual experience. The trouble with both these man-centred methodologies is that they yield no reliable or authoritative access to the knowledge of God.

Rationalism

Rationalism is inadequate for a number of reasons. First, on an a priori level, because reason can't create its own presuppositions. It's a tool, needing data to work upon. In the absence of primary information, the honest rationalist will always end up in a state of self-confessed agnosticism, rather like an inadequately programmed computer.

Secondly, it is inadequate on a philosophical level, because the very nature of God precludes his being investigated by conventional rationalistic science. Deductive logic, for instance, is inappropriate because God is the source of the universe. He's underived from anything else; he is cause, not effect. Inductive logic fails also because, being utterly unique, there is no analogy to the being of God from which inferences might be validly drawn about him. And empirical methods are useless because the whole idea of putting God in a test-tube is inconceivable, not to say impious.

Some theologians (of the Barthian or neo-orthodox school) have pushed this particular line of argument so far that they have denied that God can ever be the object of human knowledge in any respect whatsoever. I'm not defending that position, but there is no doubt there's an element of truth in it. God is the I AM, the eternal subject, and to turn him into an object of human rational enquiry is to reverse the roles. Implicitly it deifies mankind.

Those of us who accept the Bible would have an additional objection to rationalism as a theological method, and that is that fallen human reason has a congenial mental block about God. It's not that sin has destroyed human intelligence but there is a moral resistance to the truth, so that whenever a person engages in theological speculation his ideas always turn out perverted. As Paul expresses it in Romans 1:25, he exchanges the truth about God for a lie. For all these reasons then, rationalism fails as a means of knowing God with any kind of reliability or authority.

Mysticism

When we turn to the alternative of mysticism we encounter no less uncertainty and vulnerability to error. No-one, of course, can deny the reality of spiritual experience. It is part of our human heritage and it finds expression in just about every religion in the world. Sceptics can rationalize such experiences in psychological terms but Christians don't have to accept that kind of reductionism. Man is made in the image of God and he therefore has a transcendent dimension within his own psychic makeup. So mystical experience is not illusory or necessarily demonic, but is a reflection of mankind's hunger for God.

Whilst we might claim as Christians to understand human spirituality better than other people, we can never claim to monopolize it. However, even granted that mysticism is valid as experience, as a means of knowing God it is still inadequate.

It is inadequate because it lends itself to such a diversity of interpretations. By nature, mystical experience is totally subjective and non-verbal. As Arthur Koestler has put it in one of his books: 'Because the experience is inarticulate, it doesn't have any sensory shape, colour or words; it lends itself to transcription in many forms, including visions of the cross, or the goddess Kali. A genuine mystical experience,' he says, 'may mediate a bona fide conversion to practically any creed, Christianity, Buddhism, or fire-worship.'[3]

The theological meaning that is attributed to a mystical experience depends entirely on the teacher. You take your experience to a Catholic monk and he will make you a good Catholic out of it. You take it to a Sufi and he will make you a good Muslim out of it. You take it to an Indian Guru and he will make you a Hindu out of it and so on. People can be taught quite contrary ideas about God on the basis of the same mystical experience because the theological interpretation of it is an imposition on to the experience, not an extraction from it.

So when we like Zophar ask, 'Canst thou by searching find out God?' (Job 11:7, KJV) the answer is 'No'. Rationalism and mysticism fail as a means of arriving at any kind of certainty in our knowledge of God. The world by its wisdom has not known God, says Paul in 1 Corinthians 1:21. What is the solution to that impasse?

Divine revelation

I would suggest that the right Christian solution lies in the other major category of religious epistemology or knowing, namely that of divine revelation. Here the initiative lies not in man's search for God, whether via the route of reason or experience, but in God's voluntary self-disclosure to mankind. This is what lies behind my opening statement: as evangelicals we believe that our knowledge of God is primarily and supremely mediated through the *Bible*.

It is important that there are no misunderstandings at this point, so let me make four clarifications.

First, this emphasis on the Bible as the Word of God isn't to be understood as either anti-rational or anti-mystical. We accept both human reason and spiritual experience as gifts

100

of God. But the divine Word of biblical revelation possesses an authority which surpasses reason and mystical experience. It informs our reason so that our theological thinking can proceed upon a correct presuppositional basis and it interprets our experience so that we draw from it valid theological conclusions. It is the function of the Bible to control and qualify these gifts and to deliver us from the dangers of subjectivism which are implicit in both of them.

Secondly, it doesn't imply that we have no access to the knowledge of God outside the Bible. Against the extreme position adopted by some theologians, we do accept the existence of general revelation. The eternal power and deity of God are *perceptible* in the created universe. But it is important to stress that this knowledge of God is still revelatory. It is a response to God's initiative of self-expression. It is not a deduction of human logic. According to Romans 1 it belongs rather to the category of self-evident truths, of which all have a natural intuition. As Paul says, the existence of God is 'clearly seen' (Rom. 1:20). This has little to do with the so-called proofs of God's existence in which rationalistic theology in the eighteenth century, for instance, so delighted.

Thirdly, it does not imply that God's self-revelation is only a matter of the verbal inspiration of prophets and apostles. In recent years a number of theologians have emphasized the importance of redemptive *events* as the locus of divine revelation. A book by G. E. Wright written in the 1950s, *The God who Acts*, was a lucid exposé of this view.

Unlike the Muslims and the Mormons, we don't have an inspired text that floated down from heaven in some mysterious way. God's supernatural interventions in history are the anchor around which biblical revelation is focused, and this gives it an objectivity and a credibility which sets it apart from all the other religions which claim to be based on divine revelation. But revelatory events need to be interpreted, and it is precisely the function of prophet and apostle not only to tell us what God has done in history but what he means by it.

There is a fine example of this in 1 Corinthians 15:3:

'Christ died...'	*event*
'...for our sins...'	*interpretation of the event*
'...according to the Scriptures.'	*source of the interpretation*

Events only become revelatory acts of God as God himself explains them to us. And this is the chief function of the Bible; without it we're reduced to being spectators trying to make sense of a subtle TV drama where the sound volume has been turned down to zero.

The fourth thing about this proposition is that it in no way contradicts the perfection of Christ as the full and final revelation of God's person to mankind. It would be equally true, and to many people far more appealing, if we said we believe that our knowledge of God is primarily and supremely mediated through Christ. But fine and valid though such a statement would be, it would be unhelpful because it would not indicate what channel of access we who live in the 1990's have to this Christ. There are today countless bogus Christs being offered to the world. There's Christ the Hollywood superstar, Christ the anti-colonial freedom fighter, Christ the Eastern Guru, Christ the humanitarian moralist. Everybody wants Jesus to hold their banner, to represent their enthusiasm. One is tempted to say, as in that television quiz programme, 'Will the real Jesus of Nazareth please stand up?' Where are we to find him?

There is only one answer, and that is in the God-authorized documents that speak of him. In this regard we must give credit to the New Delhi World Council of

Churches conference in 1961 which revised the confessional basis of the World Council to read 'A fellowship of churches which confess the Lord Jesus Christ as God and Saviour *according to the Scriptures*'. Of course it must be 'according to the Scriptures', because there is no other Jesus to confess. Any other Jesus is an imposter. Christ coming as the Word made flesh did not supercede the need for the Bible. It made that need all the more obvious.

The divine origin of the Bible

Our knowledge of God, then, comes not by our own rationalistic or mystical insights but through divine revelation, and that revelation is found in Scripture. Scripture has been given to us as a revelation by means of verbal inspiration. There have been, of course, many attempts to escape this; the old liberal objection was that the Bible *contained* the Word of God but mixed within it a great many fallible words of men. Often it was argued that inspiration influenced the authors but not the words. The Spirit, as it were, gave them insights and ideas, albeit shadowy and imperfect, and the author was then left to try and communicate these to us as best he could within the limitations of his natural ability.

The motivation behind this liberal view is easy to understand: they wanted to do justice to the humanness of the Bible. It is obvious to anybody that the personalities of the authors shine through the books of the Bible. It cannot be said often enough, therefore, that 'inspiration' does not mean mechanical dictation. But what the liberal alternative comes down to is that the Bible can only yield its knowledge of God as it is studied by someone who is prepared to evaluate and, if necessary, reject what it says. And thus rationalism has been resurrected as the final authority, under the cloak of biblical criticism. The arbiter of truth becomes not the Bible at all, but the scholar in his assessment of the Bible's reasonability.

A more recent kind of liberal attack comes from Neo-orthodox theologians. In line with their general rejection of anything rationalistic, they argue that the Bible *becomes* the Word of God when the Christian encounters the living God through its pages. Again the motivation is in many respects laudable. Karl Barth deplored the kind of sterile orthodoxy which too often characterized traditional Protestant liberal study of the Bible, and his protest is well-founded. We must insist that merely to deduce the attributes of God from the Bible and list them in a work of systematic theology is not necessarily to have personal dealings with God at all. The Christian is one who not only knows *what* he believes but *whom* he believes.

And yet what the Barthian alternative to inspiration comes down to ultimately is that the Bible is not a book of revelation at all. It is simply the place where God, by some peculiar whim, chooses to meet people experientially, and thus mysticism has been resurrected as the means for obtaining the knowledge of God.

It is only a strong doctrine of inspiration which can defend us against the slide back towards these man-centred theological methods of rationalism and mysticism. If we're told that such a doctrine denies the humanness of the Bible, then we reply that it does nothing of the kind. And the most powerful argument, probably, that can be mustered at that point, is the analogy to the incarnation.

What happened that day in Nazareth? A fallible, sinful, human woman was so acted upon by the Holy Spirit that the child conceived in her womb was one hundred per cent human and one hundred per cent divine. He was her son and God's Son. What happened in the cases of the prophets and the apostles? The Spirit of God so acted upon them, fallible and sinful though they were, that the words they spoke were one hundred per cent human and one hundred per cent divine, human words and God's Word. Of course it is miraculous. In one case it's the miracle of the incarnation and in the other it's the miracle of inspiration. But for those who believe the one there should be no intrinsic difficulty in believing the other. Humanness and divinity are united in the Word made legible in a manner not unlike the way they united in the Word made flesh.

If we are asked for evidence of such a miraculous doctrine then we have three arguments to cite:

1. The Bible's self-testimony

'All Scripture is inspired' (2 Tim. 3:16, RSV), that is, 'breathed out by God'. If it be argued that to defend the inspiration of the Bible by quoting the Bible is a circular argument, then we reply that the validity of an *absolute* authority can only be established by argument that is in some sense circular. In the nature of the case, there is no authority *higher* than that of the Word of God to which appeal might be made for 'proof' of the Bible's divine origin.

2. The testimony of Christ

Even if we only accept that the Gospels provide us with a trustworthy account of Jesus' teaching, we are compelled to conclude either that the doctrine of inspiration is true or that Christ was mistaken. But it is quite clear that he accepted fully the Old Testament's divine authority. Well does John Bright comment in his book *The Authority of the Old Testament:*

I find it interesting and not a little odd that although

the Old Testament on occasion offends our Christian feelings, it did not apparently offend Christ's 'Christian feelings'! Could it really be that we are ethically and religiously more sensitive than he? Or is it perhaps that we do not view the Old Testament as he did?[4]

3. The testimony of the Holy Spirit

There is a lovely story of how Spurgeon used to gather crowds for open-air sermons. He would have a hat and put it down on the ground as if there was some little animal underneath it. He would point a quivering finger at it and say 'It's alive, it's alive!' Of course a crowd would gather, waiting to see what kind of animal he had got hidden under there. Then he would pick up the hat and underneath there would be a Bible. He would wave it in the air and say 'It's alive!' and start to preach.

I don't know whether it would work today. But what he said, of course, was absolutely right. When someone listens to or reads from the Bible, he is placing himself in a most precarious place, because it is alive. I remember this is exactly how I was converted. I was reading the Bible to find out what these Christians thought and to prove them all wrong. But then suddenly the tables were turned and the Word leapt up and grabbed me by the throat. The authority of the Bible lies ultimately in its self-authenticating power. The Spirit of God acts through the Word establishing its authority in people's hearts. And for that reason, of course, Scripture doesn't really need to be defended by long-winded and dusty arguments. The best way to defend it is to preach it. Spurgeon, again, says, 'Defend the Bible? I would as soon defend a lion.'

The infallibility of Scripture

So I am not ashamed of the doctrine of inspiration. The Bible neither 'contains' the Word of God, nor 'becomes' the Word of God, it *is* the Word of God. And because it is so, verbally inspired by the Holy Spirit, it is infallible. By infallible I mean that the Bible is without error in all that it affirms. That phrase 'in all that it affirms' these days needs clarification. It is not intended to be a cop-out by which errors in peripheral areas can be tolerated in the Bible. I include that phrase for two reasons.

First, in order to make clear that the Bible is infallible only when it is interpreted according to God's intention. No-one can deny that there is a hermeneutic task involved in the understanding of any group of words, not least words that comprise a variety of literary styles, written over hundreds of years, in cultures remote from our own. It's the task of hermeneutics to determine what Scripture affirms, in the confidence that what it affirms is utterly reliable and totally true.

Second, in order to make clear that I do believe that it is the Bible's intention to make affirmations. It has got a *didactic purpose:* to communicate the knowledge of God, not just as spiritual encounter, but in the form of conceptual content which can be given verbal expression in what Carl Henry delights to call 'propositional truths'.

Propositional revelation has been one of the chief targets of anti-evangelical polemic in recent years. It has become fashionable to say that the Bible contains no doctrines. Doctrine is the result of human theological reflection on the Scriptures, and neo-orthodox theologians have hammered at the point incessantly. Revelation conveys no cognitive information, they say. It is encounter not instruction. It is impossible to make God the object of human knowledge.

This insistence on propositional truth, they say, depersonalizes revelation, turns it into abstract statements, erodes the vitality of faith, reduces God to a paper idol, is bibliolatry.

To all this we reply that it is self-evident that the Bible does intend to affirm propositional truths about God. Sometimes those propositions are explicit, as in the statement, 'God is love'. Sometimes they are implicit, as in the way that the providence of God is exemplified in the book of Esther. The propositions are there and we insist that the Bible intends to teach them. Whilst it is perfectly true that man may not, dare not, make God into the object of his human, scientific investigation (since that is rationalism), there is absolutely no reason why God may not offer himself as an object of knowledge to man, and that is precisely what biblical revelation is all about. Of course that involves accommodation to our finite human understandings, but there is no reason why valid, cognitive knowledge of God is not possible if God condescends to impart it.

There is no necessary contradiction between a belief in propositional truth and a personal encounter with God. Indeed it is extremely difficult to conceive of the possibility of one without the other, if you think about it. Suppose, for instance, I claimed I'd met Julius Caesar. You might ask me, 'Well, what does he look like? What colour are his eyes? What accent did he speak with? What sort of temperament did he have?' If my reply was that I really couldn't give you any information on those points, you might reasonably question whether I'd met him at all. For what is encounter without cognitive information being imparted? Surely at that point, this Barthian objection unmasks itself as just another form of mysticism. Knowing *about* somebody is an indispensable concomitant of knowing him. Of course, mere mental assent to the affirmations of

Scripture isn't enough. But a living encounter with the true God must begin there and cannot be less than that.

In this respect the purpose of John in writing the fourth gospel is noteworthy.

'these things are written that you may believe that Jesus is the Christ, the Son of God . . .'   *propositional truth*

'. . . and that by believing you may have life in his name.'   *personal experience*

(John 20:31)

But notice the order; the propositional truth first — then the experience. John is absolutely emphatic that Christianity is not an inarticulate mystical encounter, which the Christian then proceeds to dehydrate by theological reflection into dry propositional dogma. Christianity is an experience of spiritual life that flows out of commitment to certain propositional truths about the uniqueness of Jesus.

The sufficiency of Scripture

So infallibility is not, as some people suggest these days, obscurantism about Genesis 1. It is a word that defines our whole understanding of the nature of biblical revelation as affirming true propositions rather than just communicating unverifiable mystical experience. It is a word, in my judgment, that we cannot do without.

Inspiration renders the Bible infallible and it also renders it sufficient. That is, it is complete and provides us with everything necessary for the direction of the church and the Christian. Inspired Scripture is useful 'for teaching, rebuking, correcting and training in righteousness, so that the man of God may be thoroughly equipped for every good work' (2 Tim. 3:16–17). This doesn't mean, of course, that Bible study is the only thing the Christian needs to do. But it does, surely, mean that everything Christians do should be a response to their Bible study. It doesn't mean the Bible tells us everything that we may want to know about everything. But it does contain everything we need God to tell us if we are to please him with our lives. It is sufficient, though not exhaustive.

Historically the sufficiency of Scripture has been denied in two major ways, first by the elevation of the teaching and traditions of the church to the same level of authority as the Bible, and second by the claim to new revelations which supplement or supercede the Bible. The Catholic doctrine of purgatory is an example of the former, and the book of Mormon an example of the latter.

The only response that it is possible to make to these challenges to the Bible's sufficiency is to point out that in the closing books of the New Testament era we do not find any encouragement to look for new truth, whether from popes or prophets: 'What you heard from me, keep as the pattern of sound teaching', says Paul (2 Tim. 1:13). 'The things you have heard me say in the presence of many witnesses entrust to reliable men who will also be qualified to teach others' (2 Tim. 2:2). 'Contend for the faith that was once for all entrusted to the saints' (Jude 3). We find many warnings about false prophets who will come to us, who look like sheep but are really wolves. Always the assumption seems to be of the complete revelation that needs to be guarded rather than supplemented. There is no looking forward to new revelation to come in the New Testament such as we do find in the Messianic expectation of the Old Testament.

This doctrine of Scripture, I suggest, is what defines an evangelical. The person who embraces that doctrine is someone with whom I want to enjoy fellowship and to co-operate with at the deepest possible level in extending the kingdom. I cannot do that with people who deny the authority of the Bible, because we are approaching the whole definition of Christianity from a different angle.

However, the supreme and primary role of the Bible in the Christian's knowledge of God is no longer held as tenaciously as it ought to be by some within the circle of evangelical friendship. It seems to me that some evangelicals are generating what I can only call a new Gnosticism which eschews biblical revelation in favour of direct vertical experience. Gnosticism was an early church heresy which attempted to interpret the gospel as a form of mystical enlightenment rather than an objective revelation of truth in word and history. The whole existentialist vogue in theology today promotes such a gnosticizing drift, and many, it seems to me, are moving with it. The 'spirituality of the Spirit', vital as it is, in careless hands can lead to an undermining or contradicting of the primary and supreme function of the Bible in the matter of divine revelation.

If you asked an evangelical twenty years ago, 'How does God speak today?' he would have replied unhesitatingly, 'Through the Bible'. But in some strands of the charismatic movement today, the answer would be, 'Through the Bible, yes, but also, through the contemporary gift of prophecy'. The belief is gaining ground that God still inspires individuals by his Spirit to deliver verbal messages to the church just as he inspired people in Bible times. This is a tremendous claim, with momentous theological and practical implications. The issue of contemporary prophecy calls into question the completeness and sufficiency of the Scriptures themselves and with that the whole nature of the Christian religion. Perhaps a practical example will serve to demonstrate that this is no mere academic issue.

Recently I was visiting a Christian Union. There was a time of open worship, during which charismatics in the group clearly felt at liberty to use gifts of utterance. At one point a student stood up and read a passage of Scripture. This was greeted very politely, but with little sign of excitement among the group. A little later another student stood up and offered a word of prophecy, prefacing his remarks 'Thus saith the Lord'.

Now in terms of content the oracle was quite innocuous. I had no objection to it but I didn't think really it had any greater depth than the Scripture, in fact considerably less. The response, however, from the gathered group was rapturous. Spontaneous hallelujahs and 'thank you Jesus' echoed all around the room for at least half a minute. One clearly got the impression that as far as those students were concerned this was a far more exciting and significant event than the reading of Scripture.

So what evaluation are we to give to this phenomenon of contemporary prophecy? That seems to me to be a critical question as far as evangelical unity is concerned. If we cannot find a satisfactory consensus on the status of inspired utterance within the congregation then I think the division within evangelicalism is going to grow wider and wider until we become quite different traditions of the Christian church.

Notes

1. These chapters are an edited version of an address given at Spurgeon's College in London.
2. J. I. Packer, *Knowing God* (Hodder and Stoughton, 1975).
3. Arthur Koestler, *The Invisible Writing* (Macmillan, 1954).
4. John Bright, *The Authority of the Old Testament* (SCM, 1967), pp. 77–78.

Word and Spirit: The Bible and the gift of prophecy today

II. Prophecy today

ROY CLEMENTS

There is a continuing gift of inspired insight available to the church through the ministry of the Holy Spirit, which gift, whilst not possessing the authority or nature of Scripture, ought to be given opportunity for its exercise within the church, if she is to know God fully as her living Head.

Some Christians respond to my earlier statement on the authority of Scripture by saying 'Yes, but does God still speak today? Has inspiration been totally replaced by exposition? Has the prophet been totally replaced by the Bible teacher? Or is there a continuing gift of prophecy?' The New Testament answer to the question must, I think, be affirmative. It is true that some notable scholars have argued against that view, the best known being B. B. Warfield, who held that the supernatural charismata ceased at the end of the apostolic age. To do him justice, he was reacting against the obvious excesses of Irvingite prophecy in the mid-nineteenth century. He didn't know anything of the contemporary charismatic revolution in the church and, again to do him justice, he does not try to bolster his arguments by 'proof texts' — for the fact is, there are none.

Has prophecy ceased?

Two main passages have been cited for the cessation of New Testament prophecy. One is 1 Corinthians 13:8–10 and the other is Ephesians 2:20. The first, it seems to me, is highly precarious and the second decidedly ambiguous. 1 Corinthians 13 does indeed say that prophecy 'will cease', but it seems far more likely that Paul's timetable for this, 'when perfection comes', means not the closure of the New Testament canon but the consummation of the ages. As Martyn Lloyd-Jones observed in his *Prove All Things*, to hold otherwise is to imply that we who have a complete Bible 'know fully even as we are fully known' right now and are thus in a superior position even to the apostle Paul who confessed he only 'saw darkly.' The verdict of Max Turner in an important scholarly article on the whole subject of spiritual gifts is that the 'completed canon' interpretation of 'when the perfect is come' is 'exegetically indefensible, and is not held in serious New Testament scholarship'.

The second passage is more substantial, for Paul teaches there that the church is 'built on the foundation of the apostles and prophets'. Hence, it could be argued that prophecy is a foundational institution, like the apostles, belonging only to the first generation of the church's history. However, it is far from certain that Paul is referring here to the same kind of church prophecy as we encounter in 1

Corinthians 14. Paul could be referring to the prophets of the Old Testament era, aligning them with the apostles of the New as the joint foundation of the people of God in every age.

Or since the word 'prophets' is used without the definite article, it could be that he is speaking of a single class, 'apostles and prophets', rather as he talks of 'pastors and teachers', in other words the circle of apostolic witness from whom the New Testament canon derives, including perhaps some verbally inspired but non-apostolic figures like Luke and Mark whose contribution was unique to the early church.

It seems to me that there is no compelling reason to believe that the sort of prophecy Paul speaks of in 1 Corinthians 14 has been withdrawn. Quite the opposite; our assumption must be that this passage has relevance to us in the twentieth century just as it did to Paul's original readers.

The question we must then raise, of course, is how such prophetic utterances fit in with our previous proposition about the primary and supreme function of Scripture as the Holy Spirit's organ of divine revelation. The position I would want to defend is that *this church prophecy does not possess the authority or nature of Scripture*. Like many great hymns, or Christian devotional classics, or even perhaps some parts of the apocryphal writings, it is useful to the church but it is not verbally inspired.

What is New Testament prophecy?

In a detailed study of prophecy in 1 Corinthians, Wayne Grudem produces a great deal of evidence in support of this understanding of prophecy. Most of the arguments that follow are drawn directly from this thesis.[4]

1. 'Prophecy' in New Testament times

In the inter-testamental period, Jewish literature seems clearly to have taken the line that the Old Testament canon was complete because the *nabi*, the Old Testament prophet, was no longer around. But what is interesting is that we find in the rabbinical writing all kinds of descriptions of supernatural insights and predictions which are credited to the Holy Spirit. They clearly don't take the closing of the Old Testament canon to imply that these kind of things have stopped. There were many 'revelations' which did not have the authority of God's actual words. In addition, in New Testament times the word 'prophecy' was very broad in application. It could embrace any kind of psychic awareness, ecstatic speech, clairvoyance or religious impression, so there is no necessary reason for identifying the sort of prophecy which Paul mentions in 1 Corinthians 14 with the verbally inspired canonical prophecy of the Old Testament. His language could equally well apply to some lesser form of inspired insight, such as they were familiar with both in the pagan and Judaistic world.

2. Old Testament prophet, New Testament apostle

The New Testament counterpart of the Old Testament prophet is not the New Testament prophet, it is the New Testament apostle. This is clear from several observations. First of all, the Old Testament *nabi* was not just an inspired man, he was a personally called man. Now in the New Testament this was true of the apostles, but there is no evidence that the New Testament prophets had any special sense of vocation, such as an Amos or a Paul knew.

Secondly, the Old Testament *nabi* experienced a peculiar objectivity in their inspiration which delivered them from all self-doubt, even when, as in Jeremiah's case, nobody else

116

accepted the authenticity of their words. Paul, it seems, also gives evidence of such a vigorous sense of personal conviction and authority about the revelation he had received sufficient to call down an anathema on anybody who contradicted it. But no such conviction seems to have characterized New Testament prophets. The New Testament itself draws together Old Testament prophets and New Testament apostles, perhaps in Ephesians 2:20, as I have already mentioned, certainly in 2 Peter 3:2. But nowhere is there a link established between Old Testament prophets and New Testament prophets. In fact Wayne Grudem suggests that the reason for the adoption of the title *apostle*, rather than *prophet*, for the writers of the New Testament, may have been because it was necessary to distinguish apostles from the New Testament prophets, just as the Old Testament *nabi* at certain times in the Old Testament had to be distinguished from the man who was merely a *seer* in ancient Israel.[5]

3. Constraints on New Testament prophecy

The constraints placed upon New Testament prophecy by the apostles indicate that in their view its authority was inferior both to their own words and those of the Scriptures. Consider some of the things we read in 1 Corinthians 14, for instance.

The New Testament prophets required evaluation (1 Cor. 14:29). You cannot imagine Jeremiah submitting his words to a jury.

They could be interrupted and apparently not continue (1 Cor. 14:30). You can hardly imagine anybody shutting up Amos.

They were not allowed to establish norms in the universal church. You're not the only ones the word of God has come to, says Paul in 1 Corinthians 14:36, as if to say, look, the authority of you prophets down there must not contradict what comes to you from the tradition of the apostles.

Prophets had to be subject to apostolic authority: Anybody that doesn't recognize what I'm saying must be ignored, says the apostle in 1 Corinthians 14:38. In our churches, of course, this would amount to saying that the prophet must be consciously submissive to Scripture, for that is where apostolic authority now lies.

Perhaps most significant of all is the observation that prophets could be women. It is clear from 1 Timothy 2:12 that Paul did not permit women to teach. The reason he gives for this has to do with the authority which the teaching office implied in the church. Nevertheless, it is also clear that prophets could be women in the New Testament church (1 Cor. 11:5, Acts 21:9). If that is so, then the assumption must be that there was not the same degree of authority implicit in a prophetic utterance which there was in 'teaching'.

4. Testing New Testament prophecy

Examples of New Testament prophecy in the book of Acts indicate that such utterance could be partially inaccurate, contradictory and legitimately disregarded. In Acts 21:4 and 10–11, Paul is urged through a prophetic utterance not to go up to Jerusalem although we are told in Acts 20:22 that it is the Holy Spirit who is directing him there. What is more, the details of Paul's arrest, which Agabus the prophet predicts, are wrong in a number of significant respects as a careful reading of later verses shows. It is not true that the Jews bound Paul and handed him over to the Gentiles, but rather the Gentiles delivered him out of the hands of the Jews, and the Gentile soldiers bound him. (Compare Acts 21:11 with 21: 32–33.)

According to the criteria of Old Testament prophetic evaluation, an erroneous prophecy was the mark of a false prophet (see Dt. 18:20–22). But there seems to be no suggestion that Agabus was censured in that way, even though it is quite clear, and Luke must have been conscious of the fact, that what happened was not exactly as Agabus had said. Wayne Grudem suggests that this is further evidence of the fact that there was no claim to infallibility in Agabus' prophecy, hence no possibility of people being misled by him.[6] The expectation from a New Testament prophet was quite different from that inerrancy which was expected from an Old Testament prophet in the tradition of Moses.

5. Authority of the prophet

While prophecy definitely continued in the church for a long while after the end of the apostolic age, the apostles do not see the existence of these prophets as a solution to the problem of apostolic succession. It is clear from, for example, 2 Timothy, that Paul is concerned about how the church is going to be preserved from error after his death. He emphasizes the need to guard carefully the deposit of apostolic teaching. Thus, apostolic succession is solved, not by the continuance of inspired utterance in the church, but by preservation of apostolic instruction in the church, in the form of the writings of the apostles preserved in Scripture. A New Testament prophet would not do as a substitute authority for an apostle, after the apostle's death.

The nature of New Testament prophecy

All these arguments, then, seem to indicate that 1 Corinthians 14-style prophecy is not the same kind of thing as canonical prophecy. It does not possess the nature or the authority of Scripture. But if it is not to be set on a par with

Scripture, what, then, is it?

In the past it has sometimes been identified with preaching. While I believe there is an element of truth in this, it is quite clear that the gift of prophecy Paul is describing in 1 Corinthians 14 is not preaching in the sense of expository Bible teaching. That gift is clearly distinguished in 12:28 and 14:26 and called simply 'teaching' or 'instruction'. The distinction is doubly confirmed by our previous observation that women could be prophets but not teachers. On the other hand it is also clear from 1 Corinthians 14 that prophecy fulfils many of the functions that one would associate with preaching. For instance, in verse 3 it ministers to believers, in strengthening, encouraging and comforting them. In verse 24 it is able to minister to unbelievers, bringing conviction of sin and even conversion.

The difference between prophecy and preaching seems to have been this: there was something spontaneous about New Testament prophecy. Whilst it is not true to say that the prophet lost self-control (1 Corinthians 14:32), he was prompted without notice or personal preparation, even while another prophet was speaking (1 Cor. 14:30). So prophecy was a product not of reflection on a Bible text but of sudden spiritual insight.

The Holy Spirit brought something to mind or provided some intuition, and the person thus prompted told it to the congregation, not in God's very words (like Scripture) but in his own words. It is not impossible that this may sometimes have been an emotionally charged or even ecstatic experience for the individual concerned. But this is neither certain nor necessary. For, as Paul is at pains to point out, prophecy differed from tongues in precisely this, that it was always intelligible while tongues was useless to others unless interpreted (1 Cor. 14:5). Prophecy is superior to tongues because it engages the mind of both the speaker and listener (1 Cor. 14:14–15) and so provides a more wholesome and satisfactory expression of Christian spirituality than anything which touches only the emotions. For this reason too it was able to make an impact on unbelievers present (1 Cor. 14:23–25).

In summary, prophecy seems to have been a spontaneous, intuitive insight, demanding verbal expression, but without direct derivation from the normative revelation (Old Testament or apostolic instruction) and therefore lacking the authority of Scripture though possessing edifying value.

Restoration?

But where did this prophecy go to if it was never withdrawn? Some charismatics hold a theology of last-time restoration. The gift of prophecy is Elijah returning before the last day. The charismata have been returned as a sign that the end is very close. But I personally am very suspicious of any theology which claims to give advance notice of the second coming. Those whose eschatology permits them to have countdowns to the last hour may be convinced of this sort of thing, but I can't be. It is far more likely that this gift of prophecy has always been around, but that the church has just ignored it or suppressed it, or called it by some other name.

The rigid hierarchy of the medieval church, for instance, found no place for spiritual insights from non-clerical lay people without theological education. So it syphoned off its mystics into places such as monasteries, where they couldn't threaten the establishment. In the Reformation the predominance of rationalism, I suspect, led to a similar failure to reassert this aspect of the ministry of the Holy

Spirit. A ministry of illumination of Scripture was the nearest the Puritans dared to go toward subjectivism. In more recent years the monopoly of gifts of inspiration and claims to prophecy by heretics and the lunatic fringe has further eroded its respectability. But it seems to me that among Christians who have known a personal work of the Holy Spirit in their lives one finds in every generation testimony to leadings, insights, hunches, premonitions, which are probably identical to the kind of Christian awareness that Luke in Acts regularly ascribes to the Spirit (*e.g.* 8:29; 10:19; 11:28; 13:4; 16:7; 21:4; *etc*). And when such leadings include the element of public announcement I believe they amount to what the New Testament calls 'prophecy', even if that is not what we call the phenomenon in our church tradition these days.

So what is prophecy?

I don't believe that charismatic prophecy is as new as it is sometimes said to be. You may have felt burdened at times to say something unprepared and spontaneous in the middle of a talk or Bible study. Or you may have friends who have uncanny sensitivity to spiritual things. What the charismatic movement has done is to make such spiritual intuition respectable once again in the church which for too long has been dominated by rationalistic logic and authoritarian clergy. I want to suggest that what God is doing through the charismatic movement is calling all Bible-believing Christians to give opportunity once again for the recognition of such insights as a valid expression of Christian spirituality.

In one Brethren assembly where I used to worship, there were several men who used to stand up at the morning

122

meeting, read a text because it seemed the right thing to do, and then proceed to speak. Often they completely misunderstood the text they had just read or totally ignored it. Does that mean that what they were saying was impertinent, an affront to God? Does it mean that the Holy Spirit had nothing to do with it? Or that nobody could be helped by it? Not at all. They were prophesying, not teaching. Their words had to be weighed with a great deal more critical care than exposition precisely because what they were saying was not clearly flowing out of normative revelation in Scripture. With all due respect to them, it was dangerous that they paraded it as if it did. If it had been clearly understood by the congregation that this was not teaching, but prophecy, it would have been more helpful and edifying to them.

A gift for today's church

1. The Bible commands it

Why should such 'prophetic ministry' be recognized? First, because Paul specifically encourages us to do so. 'Desire spiritual gifts, especially the gift of prophecy' (1 Cor. 14:1). 'Do not put out the Spirit's fire; do not treat prophecies with contempt' (1 Thess. 5:19–20). It is noteworthy that in his list of gifts in 1 Corinthians 12:28 Paul designates prophecy as second, above teaching. It is, of course, a moot point what the significance of that order (first, second, third and so on) is. It may well be coloured by the particular problems of Corinth and that is why tongues comes conspicuously last. But it seems to me undeniable that there is a clear New Testament directive towards the expression of this kind of Spirit-inspired insight in the church.

2. The body needs it

Secondly, we must encourage and give opportunity for such insights once again because it is a vital aspect of the church's function as a body. There is no doubt that the elevation of preaching and teaching gifts has created a clerical and intellectual elitism in the church. The ordinary unschooled person feels he has little to contribute except to make the tea and do the cleaning. But here, in prophecy, is a ministry which any believer can share in because it does not require great intellectual gifts or Bible knowledge. Here is a ministry, indeed, in which women can engage without jeopardizing our Pauline ecclesiology if that is a problem to us. For the prophet is not teaching, but offering a spiritual insight for evaluation and consideration by the rest. Nothing, it seems to me, will break down the vicious, pyramidal hierarchy and male chauvinism that still afflicts so many churches more quickly than teaching people that the Holy Spirit can lead them to make useful contributions to the spoken ministry in the church.

3. The world must see it

Thirdly, we must encourage this ministry because it demonstrates to the world that here is a God who still speaks; not in contradiction to Scripture but in a way which communicates that the Christian church is not a ministry of the dead letter but of the living Spirit. What is ultimately at stake in this whole debate is the balance between objective and subjective elements in our understanding of our relationship with God.

This tension between objectivism and subjectivism can be observed in philosophy down through every age. Our Western tradition has been heavily biased towards rationalistic objectivity and it has created atheism, the religion of the West today. The Eastern tradition has been biased towards subjectivity and has created mysticism, the religion of the East. Both these extremes are errors. Christianity has the answer. The trouble is that down through the ages the church has just been an echo of the world. In a rationalistic age we become dominated by scholasticism and deism. In a mystical age we have the anti-intellectual extremes of the charismatic movement and the existentialist theologies of Karl Barth and others. What we need is a synthesis of these characteristic Western and Eastern emphases on how we come to know things in general and God in particular.

Perhaps a simple analogy will illustrate what I mean. Think about human vision. When you look at an object, as well as seeing the detail upon which your eyes focus you also see a large surrounding area, the so-called peripheral zone. Now human knowledge, it seems to me, is a bit like that. Rationalism concentrates its gaze on things upon which the mind can focus clearly. But there is no doubt that there is a vast area of peripheral awareness which you cannot tie down in scientific terms. You may call it existential awareness, emotions, feelings, intuitions, all the things that a computer can't share with a human being. The fact that we can't bring these perceptions into rationalistic sharp focus in the same way that scientific facts can be, doesn't mean they are imaginary, any more than it is true to say that central vision is more real than peripheral. And neither is it right to draw a sharp distinction between these two types of seeing, for the fact is that they always go together and even overlap. Now it seems to me that it is this way of viewing the poles of objective and subjective knowledge, not as mutually exclusive, but more like the foci of an ellipse of total human awareness, that we need if we are to understand what it means to know God.

Word and Spirit

We need to take seriously human objectivity and human subjectivity and not play off one against the other. The Bible insists that we must come to God as persons to be recognized, and personal knowledge clearly bridges the gulf between the objective and the subjective. Of course persons are objective realities: they don't exist only in our experience. We encounter them through the gateway of objective knowledge as we see and hear them. But if we treat persons only as objects we will never really know them, even though we may know much about them. To know a person means to be subjectively involved with that person. And so it is in our knowledge of God. That is why the Bible speaks clearly of revelation in Word and Spirit.

Word . . .

Previous Western preoccupation with scientific, rationalistic knowledge has been reflected in a general emphasis amongst Christians on the importance of the Word of truth: objective revelation. The current swing toward subjectivity, in existentialism and so on, has not surprisingly been paralleled by renewed interest in the Spirit. But the Word and the Spirit cannot be separated, any more than speech can be parted from the breath that conveys it. The Bible teaches us that the personal God is encountered through the objective revelation of ordinary sense-perceptions as we see his acts and hear his words in the Bible, but *knowing about God* in this way is not the same as *knowing God himself*.

. . . and Spirit

We must go on to meet God through the Spirit, to recognize the person who stands behind these mighty acts and speaks these mighty words, and enter into a relationship with him.

Thus the Word without the Spirit is sterile. It produces only an intellectual Christianity; it may produce King Josiah's reformation (2 Chr. 34:8–33) but it will never produce Pentecostal revival. Similarly the Spirit without the Word produces no more than an incoherent mysticism that is practically indistinguishable from the dangerous intuitions of paganism. King Saul dancing naked among the prophets, vitality without order – that is the Spirit without the controlling influence of the Word. If God is to be truly known, then the Bible, it seems to me, insists that there must be this co-operation between external, revealed truth and internal, spiritual experience and intuition. We need a spirituality which takes seriously the objective revelation of God which we find in the Bible, while at the same time doing justice to intuitive, less well-focused, but experientially important feelings which arise out of our personal encounter with God through the Spirit.

We need a spirituality of Word *and* Spirit, as in Ezekiel's valley of dry bones (Ezk. 37). We need an unashamed commitment to the Bible as the supreme and primary source of our knowledge of God but also an openness to the contemporary leading of the Holy Spirit in the hearts and minds of Christian men and women.

Notes

1. B. B. Warfield, *Counterfeit Miracles* (Banner of Truth, 1972). Originally delivered as a series of lectures in 1917–18. For more recent defences of Warfield's position, see Richard Gaffin, *Perspectives on Pentecost* (Presbyterian and Reformed, 1979), Walter Chantry, *Signs of the Apostles* (Banner of Truth, 1973) and Victor Budgen, *The Charismatics and the Word of God* (Evangelical Press, 1985).

2. D. Martyn Lloyd-Jones, *Prove All Things* (Kingsway, 1985), p. 32.

3. Max Turner, 'Spiritual Gifts Then and Now', *Vox Evangelica*, XV (1985), 7–64, p. 38.

4. Wayne A. Grudem, *The Gift of Prophecy in 1 Corinthians* (University Press of America, 1982). The book is distributed in the UK by Eurospan Ltd, 3 Henrietta Street, London WC2E 8LU. See also Wayne A. Grudem, *A Gift of Prophecy* (Kingsway, 1988).

5. Grudem, 1982, pp. 43–53.

6. Grudem, 1982, pp. 79–82.

CHAPTER SEVEN

Quiet Time dynamics: What happens when we meet with God and hear his Word

STEPHEN D. EYRE

'IT'S been eight months since I had a Quiet Time . . .' That's how I began a seminar I was doing on 'How to Have a Quiet Time.' Not surprisingly, there was a notable stir in the room.

I shared that my relationship with God was reflected in my Quiet Time, or rather, in my lack of one. Before this dry spell, I had set aside several hours a day for several months to seek the Lord. Repeatedly I had called out to him to change me. When he began to answer my prayers, it was not what I was expecting. Not only my Quiet Times, but all of my life was shaken and transformed by God's work. It was a confusing period in my life, and I coped by avoiding Quiet Times altogether. God did not seem put off by this. I look back now and see that God continued to meet me and draw me in ways that I never could have anticipated.

Despite my eight-month lapse, I have found that if I am to grow in my knowledge of God, a regular discipline of meeting with God is important. Regular Quiet Times led up to my lapse and were picked up again when that important part of God's work in me was completed.

Quiet Times, devotions, or whatever we may call our practice, is a *place* and *space* we choose to create in our lives so that we can meet with God. In this age of driven and busy people, it is frequently a neglected discipline. But without a devotional practice, daily life becomes shallow and vague. With a vital devotional time, all of our lives are opened to the privilege and pleasure of God's presence.

Through a time set aside to be with God, usually in the morning, we turn our hearts to seek God and submit ourselves to do his will. In the time of quiet we create to be with God, there should be time for prayer and Bible study. Many keep a journal. The time might also include periods of silence or the singing of worship songs. Whatever we do in our Quiet Time, it is important that we open ourselves up to the benefits of the cross and enjoy the access to God that Jesus has opened up for us.

Through the years as I have practiced a Quiet Time, I have found that at times they are regular and disciplined, at other times occasional and inconsistent. At times they are rich and sweet; other times, dry and boring.

This diversity of experience no longer surprises me. My Quiet Times go through shifting phases because all that happens in my life with God is connected with my Quiet Time. Quiet Times vary widely because the work of God's Spirit in my life varies widely. Initially I felt guilty about these ebbs and flows. I don't any more. Knowing God, like knowing any other person, is an ever-changing experience.

Dynamics of knowing God

The root issue in a Quiet Time is, 'Am I meeting with God?'

One of the questions I frequently ask in counselling and discipling is, 'How is your Quiet Time?' If the person is having one, usually there is a slight pause and then the answer, 'I am having it regularly.' Or, 'I have been studying the Scriptures diligently.'

Both responses are good, but not what I am after. I want to know more than just frequency or diligence in Scripture, though both are important. What I want to know is 'What is happening in your personal encounter with God?'

Only as I get a glimpse of what's happening in the heart in touch with God can I give helpful spiritual guidance. Is there a sense of worship or a sense of deadness? Perhaps so many concerns come to mind that we can't focus on the Scriptures. Or our prayer may be jumbled and distracted. All these things mean something, indicating both our needs and what God may be doing in our hearts.

I also want to know what is happening in a Quiet Time because I have found that it is possible to be blind to the presence of God and not even know it. When this happens Quiet Times become merely an empty formality. Scripture becomes a book of principles to be applied. Prayer is a shopping list of things God is supposed to do. Difficulties in life are problems God is supposed to solve.

When we are blind to God, what God is doing in us in the midst of difficulties is overlooked. That God might want us to listen rather than do all the talking in prayer never occurs to us. And that God might want to meet us in Scripture is lost in our search for principles.

The presence of God

Is it really possible to meet with God in a Quiet Time?
Yes.

The Lord's presence is the birthright of every believer and the heart of every Quiet Time. Before Jesus was born he was named Immanuel — God with us. During his discipling of the apostles, Jesus promised them, and us, that he would not leave us as orphans but make his home with us (Jn. 14:15−21). His last words in the Gospel of Matthew were his promise to be with us to the end of the age (Mt. 28:20).

This is more than an abstract promise or an intellectual idea. Nor is it an exotic mystical experience. It is merely a matter of relationship. God intends us to know that he is with us. Meeting with God is very similar to being with a friend when you know each other well. There is a sense of connection that is much deeper than what we say to each other or the things we do together.

Sometimes you can know the presence of the Lord as a warm, quiet affection that wells up as you sit quietly before him. At other times the sense of his presence may come as a deep sense of heaviness and grief over your sinfulness. Or perhaps you know the Lord is with you as you read the Scriptures — a sense of inner nourishment as you read about God's work in the lives of people in the Old and New Testaments.

Moses knew the experience of the Lord's presence. In a very intimate encounter with God, Moses is burdened by the thought of leading Israel through forty years of wilderness wanderings. God says to Moses, 'My Presence will go with you, and I will give you rest.' Moses responds, 'If your Presence does not go with us, do not send us up from here. . . . What else will distinguish me and your

people from all the other people on the face of the earth?'
(Ex. 33:14—16).

There is a challenge to us in Moses' words. God's presence gives strength for living. And, we should note, the presence of God with us is not merely for our benefit. Others too will sense a depth about our lives that stirs spiritual hunger within them.

Spiritual perception

But when we talk about the Lord's presence, there is a problem. The experience of the Lord's presence requires spiritual perception. This is difficult because the effects of modern culture, as well as our own dullness, can make us spiritually blind and deaf. We easily become like a colour-blind person who can't see the colours red and green and doesn't really miss them. Colour-blind people know the words *red* and *green*, but have no experience of the colours. This type of blindness happens to us spiritually. We may have knowledge about God, but have no experience of God.

Because it can be so subtle, we need to pause and consider whether this 'God-blindness' is happening to us. Stop for a second and ask yourself 'How well do I see and hear the Lord?'

I discovered the dullness of my spiritual eyes and ears through keeping a journal. I began the practice of asking God questions in my journal. I would write, 'God, what do you think about . . .?' or 'What should I do about . . .?' I also just wrote down general thoughts and ideas that would come to mind.

I noticed that I would often get insights related to my questions from previous days. I would write down the insight and be pleased that I had figured out another problem.

133

However, I frequently discovered that the insight would raise another question. So, I would write that question out in the form of prayer.

One day I was reading over my journal entries for the preceding several months. It became clear that I was reading a conversation, a dialogue between two people. Someone was asking questions, and someone else was answering! It dawned on me that my brilliant insights weren't something I could claim credit for. God had been answering my questions all along, and I didn't even know it.

Discerning the Lord's presence is much like the experience of Samuel and Eli in 1 Samuel 3. The Lord spoke to Samuel several times before it became clear that God was speaking. Initially Samuel thought that Eli was calling him. In turn, Eli also initially dismissed Samuel and sent him back to bed, probably thinking that Samuel was just having a restless night. However, the third time that Lord called, old Eli began to figure out that this was God, not merely a young boy's active imagination.

Like Samuel and Eli, we need to recognize God's voice, and this can take time. We shouldn't be surprised if we don't get it right away.

Using your emotions

How can we grow in spiritual perception?

All relationships involve our emotions, and our relationship with God is no different. Just as ignoring our emotions will leave us feeling separate and distant from people, the same will be true of our relationship with God if we ignore its emotional dimension.

So if we are to grow in spiritual perception, then we need to understand that emotions play an important role. With my emotions I sense God's affection for me, embrace his Word and react to his commands.

I realize that to bring in emotions is to invite controversy. Talking about emotions among Christians can be, well, emotional. Some pride themselves on their emotional restraint. Others take pride in their ability to display emotion. For those who value emotional restraint, let me say that, while I am suggesting that we must open ourselves up to emotion, I am not necessarily advocating outward displays of emotion. For those who have found great benefit in the feeling side of faith, you should keep in mind that emotions are natural responses that vary from time to time and should not be forced or manipulated.

Both in Scripture and in history, we see godly people whose emotions were central in their encounters with God. David, as many psalms testify, experienced tremendous heights and great depths. Elijah, Jeremiah, Jonah and Habakkuk, to mention a few, had their times of ups and lots of downs.

We need to note that our emotions are more than *mere* reactions. They *mean* something. The writer of Psalm 42 begins, 'As the deer pants for streams of water, so my soul pants for you, O God.' He continues, 'Why are you downcast, O my soul? Why so disturbed within me?' (verses 1, 5).

Today we would just consider ourselves depressed. The psalmist, in contrast, knew that his soul was 'downcast' for a reason; he was thirsty for a fresh encounter with God.

Can we see emotions as helpful indicators of the spiritual life within? Do we stop to think that our down times may be more than mere depression but perhaps a sign of spiritual need?

Jonathan Edwards used the term 'religious affections' to describe our emotional responses to God. He too, valued emotions as a means of spiritual insight. Edwards wrote of 'a sense of heart wherein the mind not only speculates and beholds, but relishes and feels.'

During the First Great Awakening in New England, when critics wanted to dismiss the revival as merely excess emotions, Edwards defended it, saying that God was not interested in mildly affected worshippers. In fact, Edwards turned the table on those who were upset by all the emotional displays. He demonstrated that in Scripture *the worst possible spiritual state was a hard and unaffected heart*. What God desires are those whose hearts burn with a desire for him.

Edwards also pointed out that spiritual affections are not merely 'emotional highs.' Times of grief and mourning also come as we draw close to him and discover a need to be cleansed and purified.

A word of caution: strong emotions are not a guarantee that God's Spirit is at work. Satan can duplicate almost anything. The way to discern true spiritual affection is in our love for God. Are we growing in appreciation of God's might, majesty and beauty? And when we are emotionally down, are we pitying ourselves or are we reaching out to seek God's consolation?

We never spiritually grow beyond our emotions. I used to think my great emotional swings as a young Christian would level out as I approached spiritual maturity. I kept waiting to grow beyond my ups and downs. But after being a Christian leader in college, four years of seminary and a good number of years into ministry, my swings weren't levelling out like they were supposed to. My ups and downs weren't as unsettling as time went on. (I stopped fearing that God had left me). If anything, my feelings were more intense. But I was worried about my apparent spiritual immaturity. When was I going to grow up?

Eventually I learned that because my relationship with God is a personal encounter, I must give myself permission to *feel* — both the ups and the downs.

Once we are open to our emotions before the Lord, fresh springs of spiritual life can open up. And there is no better place to embrace our emotions/spiritual affections than in our Quiet Times.

Quiet Time phases

Because knowing God is a dynamic personal relationship, just like any other relationship, it tends to shift and vary with time and circumstances. If we are unaware of this dynamic, we may expect the same thing to happen each time we sit down to enjoy time with God. But the reality is that our Quiet Times are full of variety. Sometimes they are rich and vibrant, other times stiff and dull. Sometimes they require great determination, and other times they seem fresh and spontaneous.

If we think of Quiet Times as merely something we do, a method to be followed, then this variety will bother us. But if we know that our Quiet Times are always changing because our relationship with God is always growing and developing, then we can view these changes in our Quiet Times with deeper spiritual insight.

In my own reflections on my Quiet Times, I have discerned at least five different phases:

● Occasional Quiet Time
● Determined Quiet Time
● Study Quiet Time
● Desert Quiet Time
● Devotional Quiet Time

Each phase of Quiet Time is a reflection of spiritual

movements in our life with God. Each phase has its own characteristics and feel. Each phase has its own strengths and weakness, its own dangers and delights.

How we move through the phases of our Quiet Times depends on how God is working in us. (This is why it is not good to be judgmental of yourself, or others, about the phase of Quiet Time that you are in.) There is no formula for how to do it.

We should not expect to move through the phases in order. Nor should we expect that we would all move through each phase. During one period of your life, the work of the Spirit may express itself in a Determined Quiet Time; you find a need to take hold of your daily routine and build in Quiet Time as a regular discipline. At another point, you may shift into a Study Quiet Time in your hunger for the Scriptures. As you move along in your pilgrimage, you may enter times when your sense of the Lord becomes threatening and your heart seems to dry out; you are in the desert. On the other hand, you may find joy erupting in your Quiet Time and that your devotions are on fire.

I wish I could report that once having reached a Devotional Quiet Time I have continued on in ever-deeper emotional intimacy with God. However, this is not the case. It's as if I have a rubber band attached to my back that yanks me back whenever I am enjoying my time with the Lord, and I find that I am once again having Occasional Quiet Times. At the same time, I have discovered that every phase has an important role to play in my relationship with God. Like a swinging pendulum on a grandfather clock providing power to keep the hands of the clock moving, so the movements back and forth in our Quiet Times provide power to keep us moving forward in our pilgrimage toward heaven.

Let's consider each phase of the Quiet Time in more

detail. We can get a picture of what each phase of our Quiet Time is like as we consider the uses of Scripture, prayer, our emotions, frequency, our sense of the Lord's presence and our reasons for practising a Quiet Time as a spiritual discipline.

Occasional Quiet Time

When a Quiet Time is occasional, it means that there is no regular discipline of meeting with the Lord. (Remember, you don't have to have a Quiet Time to be a Christian. But those who have grown spiritually over the years have practised a disciplined time of meeting with the Lord.)

Because our time set aside with the Lord is not a focus or priority, Scripture reading tends to be the 'skip and dip' method. I pick up the Bible whenever I feel the need and read wherever it falls open. (My tendency is to end up in Psalms when I slip into this phase.) My Quiet Time is rather like eating on the run; I grab a sandwich, an apple or a chocolate bar as I rush through the kitchen and out of the back door.

In the Occasional phase, prayer tends to be haphazard and task-oriented. I pray only when there is a need. It's usually some version of 'Lord, help me with this.' Or, 'Lord, please do that.' For the most part, even when I do sit down to be with the Lord, there is little sense of worship. I am usually so busy inside that I can't hear (and join) the Spirit as he cries 'Abba Father' within me.

Emotionally, my response to the Lord is on-again/off-again. Sometimes I am excited about him; other times I am not. Most of the time, other things than God are on my mind and heart.

Although the Occasional phase is something most of us

go through, it is not a good place to be for very long. God is moved to the edge of our lives rather than in the centre where he belongs. We tend to see God as someone we believe in rather than as a person who is with us.

Usually there is no intention to be so casual with God; it just seems to happen. There is always one more phone call to make or one more page to read or one more urgent meeting to attend. Somehow God is moved aside in the rush of our busy schedules.

If you have spent very long in an Occasional Quiet Time, then you need to set your heart to meet with the Lord daily. You will need to be firm about it and guard your time. Don't let anything get in the way until you are established in it.

Determined Quiet Time

As the pendulum of religious experience swings, we may find that our Occasional Quiet Time has been replaced by its opposite, the Determined Quiet Time. The Determined Quiet Time is practised every morning without fail. Whereas the Occasional Quiet Time comes and goes depending on how we feel, the Determined Quiet Time is practised *regardless* of how we feel. Time is set aside each day, and each day at that time we have a Quiet Time, and nothing is allowed to get in the way.

Instead of the 'skip and dip' method of Scripture reading, there may be a formal reading plan. Perhaps you plan to read through the Bible in a year (I have found the *One Year Bible* a great help). Or you may use a devotional guide that picks up a thought from selected Scripture texts and then tells a related story with a moral.

Like Scripture reading, prayer in the Determined phase tends to follow a predetermined pattern on a daily basis.

I have one friend who has a set of prayer cards, made of five-by-seven index cards, with pictures of the people he is praying for stapled to them and with concerns listed beside the picture. He goes through them each day and has found this a great help. My practice is not so elaborate. I usually just have a list on a piece of notebook paper that I keep current, crossing out names or issues as the prayers are answered while adding new names to the bottom of the list. The advantage of having a daily, set pattern is that certain people and issues receive the benefit of our consistent prayers.

The Determined Quiet Time is a necessary phase of our spiritual walk. Intimate relationships require attention. Good friends and lovers make plans to be together. So we must make plans to be with the Lord. As I determine to set aside time to be with the Lord, to read Scripture and go through a set pattern of prayer, I am living out and reinforcing what I value most − a relationship with God. I am both spiritually strengthened and grow in my love for God.

Some of us are more disciplined than others. The Determined Quiet Time is important for me because I am not one to whom discipline comes easily. It is just like physical exercise. If we keep at our exercise, even when we don't feel like it, our body is strengthened and we look and feel better. Likewise as we spend regular time with the Lord, even when we don't feel like it, we grow in character and are enabled to live in the presence of the Lord.

There are some dangers in a Determined Quiet Time. Either we may worry about skipping a day because we fear that God will be displeased with us, or we can slip into a self-satisfied attitude about doing our daily religious duty. It is easy to place a tick on the calendar and unconsciously think, 'So much for God today; now on with other things.'

When we slip into either danger, guilt or self-satisfaction, we will lose the pleasure of God's presence. Instead of meeting with God daily because he is delightful and wonderfully fearful, we meet with him out of habit or unhealthy fear.

If our Determined Quiet Time becomes merely a duty, we become trapped in an ugly habit. Instead of a loving God, he becomes to us a task master who requires us to have a Quiet Time and who rejects us if we fail to meet the standards. When this happens, it is easy to forget that the purpose of a Quiet Time is to meet with God.

If you are trapped in a Determined Quiet Time so that it has become merely a habit, it might be good for you to skip a few Quiet Times. A couple of years ago, my prayer partner mentioned that his Quiet Times were drying up. At one point in our discussion I made a shocking suggestion: 'Stop praying so much.' I knew he was seeking the Lord and could handle my seemingly heretical suggestion. I was not surprised when a month or so later he reported a freshness in his times with the Lord.

You will find that the Lord is not a legalist, and he doesn't want you to become one either. His love for you is not based on whether or not you have a Quiet Time.

Study Quiet Time

God has given us the Scriptures as the essential means by which he makes himself known to us. So the Scriptures should be an important part of meeting with him. The key distinctive of a Study Quiet Time is the serious study of Scripture. If, say, a half-hour were set aside for a Quiet Time, at least twenty minutes of that time would be Scripture study. During a Quiet Time it would not be unusual to do an in-depth study of a passage while referring to commentaries and a Bible dictionary.

When I am in this phase, rather than reading through the Scriptures in a year, I like to get a comprehensive grasp of a book or portion of Scripture. Sometimes it will be larger books like the Gospels or Old Testament history. I've spent over a year on each of the Gospels, reading them through and studying them until I felt I knew each author's main point and how they put their books together. Or I may pick a smaller book like 1 Peter. In a month of diligent study, I generally have a grasp of the main points of the book along with some rich insights to apply to my life. Or I may pick a portion of a book, like the Sermon on the Mount. I spent a year in the Sermon on the Mount, reading it every day until I could almost recall it word for word as I took walks.

The advantage of the Study Quiet Time is that we sink our roots deep in Scripture. We provide for ourselves a rich store of spiritual truth that we can draw on throughout our lives. As we see how God works in the pages of Scripture, we learn to recognize his hand in our own lives. And as we see how people responded to God in Scripture, we are inspired – for instance, to seek God, as David did.

One danger of this phase is that after all that time in study, there is often only a little time left for prayer. Leisurely devotional worship frequently gets crowded out. Since the prayer time is cramped, it is usually short, intense and task-oriented. Prayer time easily turns into a shopping list of things God needs to do and problems he needs to solve.

It is possible in a Study Quiet Time to allow our study of Scripture to become a merely mental experience. I have found that I may be learning all kinds of information about God but that I am not necessarily encountering God. During my Study phases I have experienced times when there was a clear sense that God was calling me to turn from my in-depth study to just sit before him and worship. I found myself saying, 'Not now, God, can't you see that I am busy studying your Word?'

We must be careful, especially in this phase, about the Lord's presence. We tend to assume that because we are studying Scripture we are actually in touch with God, and that he is present with us. The Pharisees no doubt thought the same thing. Remember the question we need to ask ourselves regarding our Quiet Time, 'Am I meeting with God?'

Desert Quiet Time

Chances are you have experienced Desert Quiet Times. Whenever I get to this point in a talk on Quiet Times, I see looks of recognition all over the room. Interestingly, while Desert Quiet Times are a common experience, few of us know anything about them or what to do about them.

The Desert Quiet Time is not a pleasant experience. It's like living alone in a desert. Our Quiet Times seem to dry up. If we feel anything at all, it is an inner sense of desolation.

When we move into a Desert Quiet Time there is a temptation to think that we have done something wrong. On the contrary, frequently the cause is new spiritual growth encouraged by good Quiet Times. Surprisingly, this deeper growth can lead to dryness that we didn't expect.

When we sit down to be with God in a Desert Quiet Time, he seems absent. This longing for God and the aching sense of his absence is a common one in the Scriptures. The psalmist writes in Psalm 42, 'My tears have been my food day and night, while men say to me all day long, "Where is your God?" ' (v. 3). David cries out, 'O God, you are

144

my God, earnestly I seek you; my soul thirsts for you, my body longs for you, in a dry and weary land where there is no water' (Ps. 63:1). And in another place he cries, 'I am worn out calling for help; my throat is parched. My eyes fail, looking for my God' (Ps. 69:3).

When this happens to us, nothing we do in our Quiet Time, or in any other area of our life, seems right. There is a sawdust quality about our reading or studying of Scripture. The pleasure in study that we have known before is gone. Now the words on the page are nothing more than words.

Prayer, too, is flat. Our prayers for others seem to rise no higher than the ceiling. Worship and adoration seem mere formality; songs that we might sing are heavy and laborious.

Emotionally, there seems to be nothing inside except an aching sense of emptiness. At this point all religious affections seem gone.

Because a Desert Quiet Time requires great effort, I find that it is practised irregularly. (The reason for my eight-month lapse of Quiet Time was a Desert period.) There is both a gnawing need to meet with God and yet a frustration about his absence. This desire and frustration lead to an on-again/off-again cycle. It seems to make no difference whether we have a Quiet Time or not. If we have a Quiet Time, God seems absent. If we don't have a Quiet Time, God seems absent.

Outwardly, the Desert Quiet Time and the Occasional Quiet Time look similar. Quiet Times for both are erratic and inconsistent. But inwardly the two are extremely different. In the Occasional Quiet Time we are erratic because God is not a priority. In the Desert Quiet Time we are erratic because of an aching thirst for God that we can't seem to satisfy.

While it doesn't seem to make any difference, maintaining

a regular meeting with the Lord is important during this time – even though it will be difficult. When this phase is over, we will discover wonderful benefits. I find that many of the things I know and teach about the Lord have come from Desert Times.

David benefited and was blessed by God in the desert. He spent ten years in the desert running from Saul after God had promised David the throne. It was during that time that David learned to trust God for his promises. During that time he also developed the skills to lead the nation by leading the large community of political outcasts and soldiers who came to his side in the desert.

This Desert Time can last for a week or two, or for years. When I was in seminary I went through a period of four years where God seemed absent. I believe that God wanted my theological learning to be more than an academic experience. In the midst of this time, I began to understand why some called it 'the dark night of the soul.' Don't be discouraged if it lasts a long time; there are others who have endured even longer times of dryness.

The temptation of a Desert experience is to conclude that there is something wrong with us; perhaps we have sinned or are drifting away from the Lord. (Sin and apathy do separate us from the Lord, but that is not what I am writing about.) Or perhaps we need to read more Scripture, or pray longer, or pray differently.

In fact, for those who are seeking the Lord, Desert experiences are times in which we are being drawn closer to the Lord and he is doing a deep work in our hearts. We are being trained to lift our hearts from idols and earthly attachments. We learn that there is nothing, apart from the grace of God, that can satisfy our inner longings. We are helped to become detached from our earthly desires to look and long for God. In this age of material abundance and recreational distractions, we need the ministry of the Desert.

As we get closer to the Lord, we become overwhelmed with the sense of his holiness and our sinfulness. While it seems that we are drying up spiritually, in fact, we are being purified and cleansed. This aching dryness of the desert continues until a work of the Spirit is completed in our hearts and we once again feel the joy of being in God's presence.

While we are in a Desert Time, we should not be in a hurry to get out of it. God will lead us out when he is ready. Richard Foster writes in his book *The Celebration of Discipline*, 'Be grateful that God is lovingly drawing you away from every distraction so that you can see him. Rather than chafing and fighting, become still and wait.'

When you find yourself in the Desert, take some extended time to just sit in silence before the Lord. Don't expect or demand too much; just place yourself before him. In that quiet you will find a rest that can sustain you until this phase of your life with the Lord is over.

Devotional Quiet Time

If the goal of a Quiet Time is to meet with the Lord, then the Devotional Quiet Time is meeting with him in wide-screen Technicolor. In contrast to the Desert phase, in the Devotional Quiet Time meeting with God is a delight.

In the beginning of his confessions, Augustine writes, 'You stimulate [us] to take pleasure in praising you, because you have made us for yourself, and our hearts are restless until they can find peace in you.' In a Devotional Quiet Time, we are invited by God to enter in and enjoy this satisfying rest.

I fear that in our attempts to seek God this delight of the Lord's presence is often missed. We need to remind ourselves that spending time with God is more than a duty, or a struggle; it is a great pleasure. In the Devotional Quiet Time we enter in a special way into this pleasure.

The way we handle Scripture in a Devotional Quiet Time is frequently different from conventional study of Scripture. In contrast to looking for new information or significant details of a passage, our time in Scripture has a reverent and worshipful tone.

I find it important to turn to passages that I have already studied in some depth. I spend time chewing over a passage and letting my soul soak in a passage until, with Paul in Ephesians, I marvel at the spiritual blessings that have been given to us through Jesus; or with Peter, I experience the unspeakable joy that I am receiving the goal of my faith, the salvation of my soul.

Sometimes it is helpful to picture yourself in the passage, using your imagination to enter into it – feeling, smelling and hearing what is happening. Psalm 23 is a favourite of mine to handle in this way. I imagine myself in a restful green pasture, with the sun shining warmly on me, the blue sky full of drifting white clouds and a few large trees that provide just the right shade. I find myself alone with the Lord, away from the pressures that pull at me. As I settle down (and it takes me awhile to settle), I find an assurance that the Lord is indeed present. Along with David I know the reality of the Lord who is restoring my soul.

But meditating on Scripture does not fill all of my time – it is just a part. Frequently prayer is woven into meditation on the Scriptures. Prayer in the Devotional Quiet Time is rich and varied. There is less of a task-orientation; there are fewer lists that we reel off for God to accomplish. While our prayers will include intercession, there will be times of quiet listening as well. I find less than half of my prayer time is taken up with petitions and intercession during such Devotional times. Such prayer is important for us because, in our task-oriented age, we often ask too much of the Lord too soon. We are busy with intercession and can miss the pleasure of just being with him.

I find that there is frequently a full silence in this Devotional Time, just like when I am with someone with whom no words are necessary. I have been delighted to read of Joyce Huggett's experience in *Listening To God*:

> What I heard in those times of listening was more than a voice. It was a presence. Yes. I heard the Lord call my name. But I also 'heard' his tenderness. I soaked up his love. . . . I had never delighted in God in this way before. And it had never occurred to me that God wanted me to linger in his presence so that he could show me that he delighted in me.

While not necessarily boisterous, the Devotional Quiet Time is a time full of emotions. There is a longing hunger for the Lord and, simultaneously, a sense of being filled. You may even feel a pulling on your heart that draws you to the Lord, a calling out that doesn't cease but only increases at his touch. Often there is a sense of warmth, love and joy. Not infrequently, there are times of anger and even fear. In all of the time there is a strong sense of the presence of God. You know that he is with you.

The Devotional Quiet Time generally consumes more time than other types of Quiet Times. There is a leisure that is required to be with the Lord in this way. Somehow five minutes turn to fifteen minutes and then even to an hour.

This sense of unhurried leisure may be uncomfortable as you first enter into such a Devotional Quiet Time. You may wonder if you are merely wasting time. Perhaps you think you should be doing something more productive. As this happens, stop to remind yourself of the eternal value of being with God. If you resist the demanding voices, gradually such pressures won't seem so insistent.

When you think about the time a Devotional Quiet Time requires, it becomes clear why we don't experience the pleasure of the Lord in this way as often as we might. Our busy lifestyles don't lend themselves to the unhurried time that a Devotional Quiet Time requires.

Like the Determined and the Study Quiet Times, the Devotional Quiet Time is practised on a regular basis — perhaps not every day, but several times during the week. You may take an hour or two one day and then only brief times for the next couple of days. Breaking of routine has little effect because of the strong, satisfying desire to be with God.

While all of us are called by God into such times of devotion, initially we may not know how to respond. As far back as the early years of my walk, I remember times when I sensed a calling in my spirit to enter into times of devotion. I wasn't sure what was happening; I didn't trust my feelings, and I had yet to hear teaching on the subject of a devotional life.

Eventually, I found devotional guides and books on spirituality to be helpful companions. The classic *The Imitation of Christ* by Thomas à Kempis is a great encouragement. While not exactly a devotional guide, *Religious Affections* by Jonathan Edwards provides rich insights and solid biblical teaching on the work of the Spirit in our hearts. Richard Foster's booklet *Meditative Prayer* and his *Celebration of Discipline* have provided signposts and markers for my journey.

While the Devotional Quiet Time is the most delightful,

I have discovered that I don't stay there. In the period of a year or two, I move back and forth from the Occasional Quiet Time to a Devotional Time. Along the way I usually hit every stage in between.

A word of caution about Devotional Quiet Times: as strange as it may sound, a Devotional Quiet Time may not always be the best for us!

In my initial enthusiasm for the delightful taste of God's presence I was discovering in fresh Devotional Times, I sought to open up people to the joys of listening to God. I was surprised at the results. Some people were enriched; some were not. I discovered that unless a person had a desire to meet the Lord in this way, the pursuit of devotion stirred up emotions and expectations they weren't prepared to handle.

Further, I discovered that continuing in a Devotional Quiet Time wasn't always appropriate. Like the disciples at the Mount of Transfiguration, it wasn't right to build shelters on the mount and dwell there. The disciples had to follow Jesus back down the mount and face the needs of the waiting crowds; and then it was on to Jerusalem and the cross.

We too have to come down from the mount. With regret, I've found that I can't expect, or demand, such divine pleasure of devotion all the time. Sometimes God gives us that delightful and deep sense of worship; sometimes he doesn't. God doesn't show up on cue, nor does he come to us in ways that we demand. He knows what we need and comes to us in ways that we can handle. The enduring reality of such pleasure in worship won't come until we see the Lord in heaven.

Temperament

Our temperaments have a great deal to do with our spiritual disciplines. I have observed that people who are methodical and detail-oriented — accountants and engineers, for example — may have a hard time getting beyond the Determined Quiet Time, focusing on rigorously doing one's spiritual duty. On the other hand, those who tend to be spontaneous — say, artists, musicians and designers — may skip the Determined phase altogether, perhaps settling in a Study Quiet Time for a while and then slipping back into an Occasional Quiet Time.

I am of the spontaneous temperament. I don't like to settle into one way of doing things for very long. I have a natural inclination to avoid set daily Quiet Times. I deal with this tendency in two ways. Sometimes I find it necessary to be very determined on a daily basis. At other times, I make it a goal to have four or five Quiet Times during the week and feel good about it if I have three or four.

Whatever our Quiet Time experience, there is no place for self-condemnation or pride. When we do well, it is surely a gift of his grace to us. When we do poorly, being either irregular or legalistic, we shouldn't be surprised. God isn't. I don't condemn myself when I miss the mark. I am grateful for what times I have. I know the Lord is glad to be with me, and I determine to do better next time.

Each person has to move through the spiritual journey in his or her own way. Wherever we are in our spiritual lives, we should keep in mind that our goal in having a Quiet Time is to live with a heart-sense of devotion in the presence of God.

Inexpressible joy

As we seek to grow in our Quiet Times, we must keep in mind that spiritual growth is a combination of God's initiative and our response. We can ignore, if we choose, the voice of the Spirit in our souls and his shaping of our lives. We can continue to live busy lives and banish God to the edges of our lives, to the borders of consciousness. If we choose to do so, we will remain in Occasional Quiet Time, thinking of God here and there and dashing off prayers in a haphazard way. If that is our response to God, our spiritual lives will remain shallow.

Or we can be people who respond to his inner workings and find ourselves being drawn to him. We will sense a pull and a call inviting us deeper. As the psalmist wrote in Psalm 42, 'Deep calls to deep in the roar of your waterfalls' (verse 7). As we sense this pull on our hearts, it is up to us to follow. We will find that as we grow in our responsiveness, he moves us through the cycles of our souls.

In her book *Many Waters*, Madeleine L'Engle, one of my favourite authors, writes about two teenagers who mistakenly disturb their father's scientific experiment and are transported back to Noah's time, just before the flood.

What I found fascinating about the story is that while the teenagers meet people, like Noah and Lamech, who have experiences with God, the two boys never have these experiences. They only hear about what God has said to others. Occasionally they wonder about this strange person called EL, but they never personally meet him.

In light of the spiritually blinding effects of this culture, I fear that there are many of us who, like the two teenagers, spend time in the Scriptures, have Quiet Times, but don't live in God's presence. We are seduced by the way we live our lives into being content just to read about him in the

Scriptures, read about him in books written by other Christians and merely do our religious duty.

Quiet Times are so much more than a duty. A Quiet Time is a divine encounter. God is with us. The purpose of a Quiet Time is to meet him. If we are not listening for him, if we are not looking for him, we may miss the meeting.

On the other hand, if we are looking and listening through carefully developed spiritual disciplines, we will, in the words of Peter, be 'filled with an inexpressible and glorious joy' (1 Pet. 1:8).

The Lord is present in his world, and all creation declares his glory. In our work, our family, our recreation, whatever we do, we can be filled with a sense of his presence.

However, unless we practise the discipline of a Quiet Time, we will be apt to miss his glory that swirls and sings around us. A fruitful Quiet Time will allow us to be before him in such a way that we sense his presence in everything we do.

Characteristics of Quiet Time phases

	Occasional	Determined	Study	Desert	Devotional
Scripture	skip and dip	a regular routine	primary focus	dry	leisurely meditation
Prayer	brief, hurried, task-oriented	intercessions, thanksgiving	intercessions, thanksgiving	empty, forced	listening silence, intercession, worship
Emotions	up and down	satisfied	satisfied	flat, frustrated	longing hunger satisfied, fear/joy, warmth
Frequency	once in a while	regular	regular	periodic	regular
Danger	God is not the centre	legalism, complacency	academic, little time for prayer	giving up	wanting to stay there
Benefits	better than nothing	developing discipline	growth in Scripture	detached from desires	enjoying God

About the contributors

John White, a psychiatrist, is a bestselling writer and speaker with a world-wide ministry.

John Balchin is a Baptist minister in Purley, south of London, and formerly lectured in New Testament at London Bible College.

Roy Clements is minister of Eden Baptist Church, Cambridge, and author of several books including *When God's Patience Runs Out: The Truth of Amos for Today* (IVP, 1988).

Jack Kuhatschek is Bible Study Editor for InterVarsity Press in the United States and author of *Taking the Guesswork Out of Applying the Bible* (IVP/USA, 1990).

Stephen D. Eyre is author of *Defeating the Dragons of the World* (IVP/USA) and a staff worker for InterVarsity Christian Fellowship, currently working among American students in Britain.

Further reading

The Bible Speaks Today series on many OT and NT books (IVP).

Growing with God, ed. Ro Willoughby (IVP, 1988).

How to Read series on types of biblical literature (IVP).

How to Read the Bible for All Its Worth, Gordon D. Fee and Douglas Stuart (Scripture Union, 1983).

Illustrated Bible Dictionary, ed. N. Hillyer (IVP, 1980).

The Lion Handbook to the Bible (Lion, 1983).

Meeting with God, ed. Ro Willoughby (IVP, 1987).

New Bible Atlas, ed. J. J. Bimson and J. P. Kane (IVP/Lion, 1985).

New Bible Commentary, rev. ed. D. Guthrie (IVP, 1970).

New Bible Dictionary, rev. ed. N. Hillyer (IVP, 1982).

Search the Scriptures, (IVP, 5th edn. 1967).

Scripture Union Notes, available from Scripture Union, 130 City Road, London EC1V 2NJ.

Tyndale Commentaries on many OT and all NT books (IVP).

Understanding the Bible, John Stott (Scripture Union, 1984).